I Hate Presentations

I Hate Presentations

James Caplin

CAPSTONE
be inspired!

John Wiley & Sons, Ltd

First published in 2008 by   Capstone Publishing Ltd. (a Wiley Company)
The Atrium, Southern Gate, Chichester, PO19 8SQ, UK.
www.wileyeurope.com

Email (for orders and customer service enquires): cs-books@wiley.co.uk

Other Wiley Editorial Offices

John Wiley & Sons Inc., 111 River Street, Hoboken, NJ 07030, USA
Jossey-Bass, 989 Market Street, San Francisco, CA 94103-1741, USA
Wiley-VCH Verlag GmbH, Boschstr. 12, D-69469 Weinheim, Germany
John Wiley & Sons Australia Ltd, 42 McDougall Street, Milton, Queensland 4064, Australia
John Wiley & Sons (Asia) Pte Ltd, 2 Clementi Loop #02-01, Jin Xing Distripark, Singapore 129809
John Wiley & Sons Canada Ltd, 22 Worcester Road, Etobicoke, Ontario, Canada M9W 1L1

Wiley also publishes its books in a variety of electronic formats. Some content that appears in print may not be available in electronic books.

A catalogue record for this book is available from the British Library and the Library of Congress.

Library of Congress Cataloging-in-Publication Data

Caplin, James.
   I hate presentations : transform the way you present with a fresh and powerful approach / James Caplin.
      p. cm.
   Includes index.
   ISBN 978-1-84112-809-2 (pbk. : alk. paper)
1.   Business presentations.   I. Title.
   Hf5718.22.C367 2008
   658.4'52—dc22

                                   2008001333

Typeset in 11/15 pt New Baskerville by Thomson Digital

Printed by TJ International Ltd, Padstow, Cornwall, UK

Substantial discounts on bulk quantities of Capstone Books are available to corporations, professional associations and other organizations. For details telephone John Wiley & Sons on (+44) 1243-770441, fax (+44) 1243 770571 or email corporatedevelopment@wiley.co.uk

CONTENTS

INTRODUCTION

The aim of this book is to help you become better at preparing and doing presentations. There is a secondary aim. This is to be part of the process of ridding the world of poor presentations, so that we all have to suffer through fewer of them in future.

My belief is that, once you start doing really good presentations – ones that deliver – people will notice. You will benefit, personally and in terms of your career, and others around you will begin to improve the way they do presentations too. That will help make you happier, will speed the flow of information in your business world, and will actually begin to change the whole of your work for the better.

What qualifies me to write such a book?

My professional background, way back, is as a writer of corporate videos. I did the job for two decades. For those too young to remember them, corporate videos used to be produced when someone with some clout and budget wanted to communicate something complicated. To do this, they would often commission 'a video', which all too often ended up as dull, over-blown and too long. They were generally despised by those who watched them. Ring any bells? Yes, they were the PowerPoint presentations of their day.

Personally, I had quite a successful career, partly because my scripts – and the videos that were made from them – were untypical. They tended to be short and intense. As an audience, you were plunged into them, told what you need-ed to know, and then released as quickly as possible.

But, in my mid-forties, I decided I wanted to do something more satisfying. While I was trying to discover what that might be, someone asked me to help them prepare a presentation – something I'd never done, but thought couldn't be that hard. I took my client through how I approached writing a corporate video, which was a revelation to her. She used the same approach to prepare her presentation. The result delighted her, and her audience. It delighted me too, because I had loved helping her, loved not writing, loved see-ing her grow in understanding of how communication works. I'd found my vocation – as a coach.

The more people I coached, the more often I came across powerful negative feelings towards presentations. I began to run *I Hate Presentations* workshops and coaching groups, dur-ing which much of what is in this book evolved. Delegates often asked me if I'd ever written anything about the subject in detail. I hadn't, but here it is now.

I Hate Presentations is a practical book. It contains no academic arguments, footnotes or extensive reading lists. Put into practice what you read here, and the way you approach and do presentations – and other communications – will never be the same again.

About Presentations

1

Aren't most presentations AWFUL? You sit there as someone drones on, with PowerPoint slide after PowerPoint slide, simultaneously apparently trying to prove they are clever, know lots about the subject they are presenting on, and at the same time bore you into submission.

And preparing presentations just adds to the stress of already busy work lives. You have to sort out what you are going to say, probably produce some slides and perhaps handouts and – in the end – the audience don't even really seem to listen.

When you do a presentation, it is nerve-wracking. Will it work? Are you going to say the right thing? Should you be putting in more jokes? More facts? More evidence? Or less jokes, facts and evidence . . . or . . . whatever?

Almost everyone in today's workplace feels at least some of these feelings – many of us feel them all. Here's the good news: it need not be like this. This book will help you do presentations in the workplace more easily, prepare them more quickly – and have lots more fun doing so. Your presentations will deliver better results, for you, your audiences, your team, business and career.

To get to that point, we first have to clear away some common misconceptions. Then, we need to do a little theoretical groundwork. Finally, we will replace those misconceptions with some ideas that work.

The first misconception is that presentations are a form of public speaking.

PRESENTATIONS AND PUBLIC SPEAKING

Who are your audience when you're doing a presentation? For most of us, it's colleagues, partners, associates, bosses, customers or prospective customers. Who are the audience for a public speaker? It is, as the words make clear, the public. *Big difference.* And the most important difference is that the public do not know much about what the public speaker is talking about. That's why they have come to hear the speech. When you're doing a presentation, on the other hand, your audience tend to be very knowledgeable about the subject, or at least the subject area. That's why they've been invited. After all, you wouldn't do a team briefing to people who weren't in your team, or a project update to those who were not involved, in some way, in the project.

Where do you do a presentation? Usually, in your workplace – or someone else's. Often it's in a meeting room, precisely so you can say things to your audience that you may not want anyone else to hear. What is the venue for public speaking? It's precisely that – in public. The speaker is on a stage, usually with a microphone, sometimes behind a lectern. Is that how you do presentations in your meetings? Most of us don't – we do them round a table.

At the end of a speech, it is convention that the audience applaud. Is that the conventional, or even desirable, response to the end of an everyday presentation in your workplace? You do a project update to your bosses, and they start to clap? And a speech has to be a certain length, long enough to make it worth the audience turning up. A presentation only needs to be as long as it needs to be.

These differences between speeches and presentations exist because one is a *broadcast* communication, the other *narrow-cast*.

Broadcasting and narrow-casting

'Broadcasting' is what the old-style main television channels do: send out a message to anyone and everyone. When broadcasting you have to cater to the lowest common denominator, i.e. take into account that Granny and the kids may be watching. To do it well you:

- Avoid jargon, as the broad audience may not understand it.
- Pace the flow of information slowly. You communicate nothing too taxing, nothing complicated, keep repeating points you've made.
- Add broad humour where possible.

'Narrow-casting' is what MTV, QVC, blogs and many modern means of communication do (it's also what corporate video does). Narrow-casters send their messages out to a narrowly defined audience. To do it well you:

- Embrace the language of the group you are communicating to. On MTV, that means presenters who talk, move, act and even appear to think like members of their audience.
- Pack in the information densely – you are talking amongst yourselves, as experts. This means assuming the audience understands the subject and talking at their level, making no concessions to Granny or the kids.
- Humour may be a help, but is not essential.

Narrow-casting is boring to those who are not in the target audience but, when done well, compelling to those who are.

How do presentations fit into this scheme?

What is a presentation?
To me, a presentation is *any* oral communication you have time to prepare, and where you are required to speak on the subject before others do. It's as simple as that.

That definition covers speeches, so what I'm actually claiming is that speeches are a form of presentation, but that not all presentations are speeches. (That may sound odd, but is no odder than the statement that while all red-headed boys are people, not all people are red-headed boys.)

The difference is that presentations are a form of narrowcast communication, and speeches are a form of broadcast communication. Presentations are done to a narrowly defined audience, who are knowledgeable about the subject and want – expect – a dense flow of information. What we all too often get is a broadcast communication: dilute, general, designed to be understood by anyone. And because of the way the world of work is developing, we are all doing more and more of these presentations; being good at them is ever more crucial if we are to thrive.

THE MODERN WORLD OF WORK

Because of downsizing and outsourcing, spin-outs and spin-offs, and the complex nature of modern projects, almost all of our work now involves collaborating with others, in cross-functional teams – often across physical borders – with people in our companies and other companies and also with associates, partners, contractors, consultants and others. To keep projects on track, and everyone involved understanding what is happening, we all have to continually do, and attend, meetings. And at those meetings, a lot of what goes on is us telling them what we are doing, and them telling us what they are doing. So we are all now doing and attending presentations. Lots of them. Continually. Day in, day out.

Think of the amount of time in each company that is wasted if these presentations are done ineptly. Think about the increase in efficiency and improvement in the way information flows through a business if they are done well. I've asked many of those I coach to estimate how often they do presentations. The astonishing average is at least one per day. So, what makes a good, everyday, workplace presentation?

Good presentations
In *I Hate Presentations* workshops, I ask delegates to describe a good presentation. The answers are surprisingly consistent. Before you read on, take a moment to formulate an answer yourself.

Delegates say good presentations:

- Capture your interest.
- Are relevant to you, the audience, and say something useful to you.
- Are concise, containing everything that needs to be there, without waffle.

I hope that corresponds, at least to some extent, with what you feel.

So, what is a bad presentation – the kind we all hate, the kind that impedes the smooth flow of business?

Bad presentations

Think about a bad presentation you have experienced as a member of the audience, and take a moment to form an answer in your mind before you read on. When I ask people in workshops this question, I again get a surprisingly consistent reaction. What they say, when you boil it down, is that bad presentations:

- Are irrelevant.
- Ramble
- Contain too much detail.

Consequently, they are boring. I hope that this too corresponds, at least to some extent, with what you feel.

Compare the demands on a speech-maker with the description of a bad presentation.

- A speech has to be full of basic information because the audience do not know much about the subject. So a presentation done as a form of speech is full of irrelevant information that the audience already know.
- A speech has to be long enough to be substantial. So a presentation done as a form of speech tends to go on and on. In other words, it often rambles.
- A person doing a speech has to show that they know about the subject they are talking about. So a presentation done as a form of speech often contains too much detail.

In other words, attempting to do a speech when actually doing a presentation is almost bound to turn out badly. Which brings us to the first 'Action Step' of this book. These action steps – which will crop up regularly – are, as the words imply, suggestions for you to do something.

Action Step: Stop making speeches
This is actually an inaction step. It is that, from now on, you are not going to think about making speeches when you do a presentation. You are going to forget anything you may have read, learnt or been trained to do that relates to speech-making as it applies to presentations.

At this point in workshops, I often notice people relax a little. The idea that you don't have to make a speech when you are doing a presentation offers a release from an onerous burden.

As part of that shift – from presentation as mini-speech, to presentation as a communication form in its own right – I always refer to the person doing a presentation as 'the presenter'. Never 'the speaker'. 'Speakers', to me, do speeches.

Let's move on. How do you, at the moment, prepare presentations? Formulate an answer before reading on.

HOW YOU CURRENTLY PREPARE PRESENTATIONS

People in my workshops respond to this question with the following, or some variation of it. First, they think about the subject, what they're going to talk about. Then, they do some research: perhaps on the Internet, in dictionaries, looking up facts and figures, reading their files. Then they write something, add PowerPoint slides, check it and finally, when they are reasonably satisfied with what they have prepared, deliver it.

A few people do other forms of preparation. There is the ignore-it-till-the-last-minute-and-wing-it technique. This occasionally works, but is high risk. Another is to take a previous presentation that worked and use search-and-replace and cut-and-paste to customize it. We'll see in Chapter 4 (the section entitled 'The importance of your first time') why this almost certainly produces a poor presentation.

Let's return to the standard preparation technique. What it boils down to is this:

1. Think about the title.
2. Research.
3. Write.
4. Deliver.

Where and when in your life did you first encounter that technique? If you don't immediately know, read through the summary again and listen for the inner voice of recognition. Because it is shockingly universal. The technique is how we were taught to do essays at school. We take it so much for granted that this is the way to create a piece of writing, that we are not aware that it is actually a learned technique. The truth is, you don't have to create a piece of writing this way. It's just how children do it. I call it the School Essay Technique, which brings us to the second Action Step.

Action Step: Stop using the School Essay Technique

I'd like to challenge you not to write a school essay for the next presentation you do. In fact, not to write a 'script' at all unless you are keen to do so. Instead, trust your mind – and the techniques I'll show you – and deliver it as you would a joke, story or anecdote. You know lots about this stuff. Trust yourself.

Let's take this thought one stage further. Is it necessary – or even useful – to write a presentation at all?

The trouble with writing

Have you ever considered the process of writing? It is astoundingly complicated. You have a thought. Quite what that means is mysterious, but somehow, something crystallizes in your consciousness. You then put vague mental words to that thought. If you are going to write, you have to listen to your mental voice saying the words, and translate what you hear mentally into action (moving your hand in some way to record the words).

To check what you've written, which most of us do as we write, you have to do the whole malarkey again, only backwards. Your eyes take in the text words, read them aloud in your head, then you have to listen to and evaluate the inner voice to see if what it is saying corresponds to the vague thought that started the whole train of events in the first place.

With all that going on, is it any wonder that most of us, when we start to write, end up with something on paper that is other than our natural voice? The untrained writer's voice-on-paper tends to be stilted and formal. That's why perfectly normal people who talk in a pleasant way write letters that start:

Dear Sir
Re 1 Acacia Avenue
Concerning the aforementioned property, please note the following three points.

'Re'? Yes, I know it's Latin, and it's legalese, but please.

'Concerning'? What sort of word is that?

'Aforementioned'?!? When do you ever say that? And why the weird, backwards word order?

Writing something to present verbally to others is a particular skill, exercised by a particular breed of crafts people called . . . 'scriptwriters'. Scriptwriters are comfortable writing dialogue. Most regular people are not.

Which brings us to the first 'Stretch'. Stretches are suggestions for how you might take the ideas in this book and apply them beyond the narrow confines of presentations. They act a bit like painting the walls and sanding the floors in the film *Karate Kid*. For those who haven't seen it, a young karate student asks a master to help him improve his technique. The master orders him to paint a huge wall and sand some floors. Eventually the boy rebels from this menial work. At which point, the master demonstrates how the repetitive movements the boy's been doing have actually trained his muscles, and his karate is already much improved.

Doing these stretches works like that. As you experiment with doing mundane tasks in a new way, you will simultaneously be learning new ways to approach presentations.

Stretch

Write some of your emails as if you were speaking them. Do not send them immediately, but put them in Drafts. Open them an hour or two after first writing them, and read them back to yourself. Do they seem like the way you speak? If not, amend them and go round the loop again. If they do, and they say what you want them to, send them.

Note what effect this has on those who get these emails, if any. Note also what this does to the way you write other documents in the workplace.

If you don't have to draft an essay or even write a script when doing an everyday presentation, what do you have to do? In order to answer that question, we first have to attend to the meaning of a presentation.

Meaning

The meaning of what someone communicates may be very different from what they say. Consider this example: Dolores is a fine young woman – intelligent, sociable, popular, attractive. And temporarily unattached. Brad wants to go out with her. He asks for a date with her this Saturday. She's busy then. How about next Saturday? Busy then too. How about the Saturday after that? Er, this is a busy period, what with preparing for exams, and family commitments, and the voluntary work she does. So, no.

Let's stop there.

Put yourself into Brad's shoes and listen to this exchange hearing only the literal meaning of the words. This is, by the way, something all too many young, and some not-so-young, men actually seem to do. What do you hear?

All Dolores actually *says* is that she's busy this Saturday, next Saturday and the one afterwards. If that's all Brad hears, what is the obvious thing for him to do? Ask for a date four weeks from now, of course – after the exams are over! Is he likely to get a 'yes'? Personally, I don't think so.

Now, listen to the words and try to make sense of them as a whole. Again, resist the temptation to go deeper. At this level, Brad hears that Dolores has a busy life. That makes sense. After all, she's an attractive person. That's one of the reasons Brad wants a date with her. She has a commitment to school and family and charitable work. That makes sense too: she's bright, loyal and has a good heart. That too is why Brad wants a date with her. So, listening at this level, Brad might not keep pestering her, but will not give up. He might say something like: 'Why don't you call me when you have some free time?' Guys who try this technique know the response is often something along the lines of 'Sure. Give me your number and I'll call.' Should Brad wait long for her call? Those of us who are old in the ways of the world suspect that it could be a long, long, long wait.

And finally, what does Dolores probably mean? Isn't it '*I don't want to go on a date with you*'?

But here's the weird thing. Dolores never actually says those words. She apologizes. She seems kind. The meaning lurks below the surface, informing everything she says, but never actually surfacing.

These three levels of listening can be represented visually:

Hearing
↓
Listening
↓
Meaning

At the top level is 'hearing'. If you listen at this level, you listen only to the words people say.

The next level is 'listening'. This can be thought of as listening to everything people say and extracting one hundred per cent of the information in the words. It's what people mean when they say someone is a good listener. A good listener in this sense doesn't interrupt, looks interested and goes 'uh-huh' a lot.

Understanding 'meaning' involves picking up the true, underlying content of the communication. It requires the listener to work quite hard. It is something most of us do instinctively some of the time, and not at others.

What would happen if Brad were to understand the meaning of the message Dolores is attempting to communicate? There are many alternatives. He could, for instance, find someone who DOES want to go out with him. Alternatively, if he is still keen to get a date with Dolores, he could find out more about her. What charitable cause, for instance, does she support? Perhaps she's a committed environmentalist. Brad could start to become interested in the environment himself. That could lead to a conversation with her on something she's interested in. Will it lead to a date? Perhaps not, but he will, at least, have a meaningful interaction with her, and who knows where that will lead?

And that is one of the big truths of life. If you stay at the hearing level, life will be constantly puzzling and frustrating. If you learn to operate at the meaning level, you will be far more effective.

This model of how people communicate has profound implications for presentations. For a start, it is another reason the School Essay Technique fails.

The meaning of a school essay

Every school essay has the same fundamental meaning. It is 'I know about this subject. Please give me a pass mark.' It is also 'I've done enough work to get a pass mark.' If you are an eager pupil, it might also be 'I've done so much work, please give me a high mark.'

Compare the meaning of a school essay as set out above with the description of a bad presentation.

Meaning of a school essay	Bad presentation
I know about this subject. Please give me a pass mark.	Which means that presentations written as school essays are full of . . . irrelevant information.
I've done enough work to get a pass mark.	Which means that presentations written as school essays . . . contain more than the minimum, so tend to ramble.
I've done so much work, please give me a high mark.	Which means that presentations written as school essays . . . contain too much detail.

In other words, using the School Essay Technique is a further *cause* of the sort of presentations we all hate. The presenter gives you lots of 'interesting' facts and figures, quotes authorities, presents high-falutin' theories. Yawn. And remember another major truth about school essays. It is irrelevant if you could complete your essay in a single, brilliant paragraph. If you don't write enough, you won't get a good mark. Short and sweet does not cut it.

The idea that school essays are not only irrelevant for presentations, but actually harmful, helps explain the feeling of dread so many people have when they prepare a presentation. If they are using the School Essay Technique, as they start working on their preparation they are likely to wonder if this will work. They are entirely correct to do so, because it probably won't. But, if the School Essay Technique is all they know, what else can they do?

So they plough on. But as they work harder at the essay they are constructing, their feeling of unease mounts. They *know* they are doing something wrong – but what is it? If they stop writing the essay, it'll be incomplete – and that's no good. If they make it better (which, for a school essay, means longer, with more facts), that's no good either. So, whichever of those you do, the feeling of dread will build, because you are still doing the wrong thing, and you are still correct to feel uneasy.

And then you are doing it.

'Hi, I'm here today to tell you about how we are going to tackle the resource limitations we have in terms of personnel as it affects our financial overview team on the Insurance and Warranty side of the business.'

Phumf! The lights go out in the audience's eyes. They try to pretend to be interested – partly so you don't burst into tears – but you know they've gone away. And you are stuck there, the centre of attention, with 20 more minutes and over 40 slides to go.

No wonder so many people hate doing presentations.

A CASE STUDY

I was coaching a marketing executive in a large company. His boss, the Director of Marketing, hired me to help Dave become more of a heavyweight Dave.

Dave did marvellous work on his communications and his status in the workplace was changing rapidly for the better. Then he got a shock. He reported to me that his boss had been called in to the MD's office and told his services were no longer required. Dave was next in. He expected the same treatment, only to be offered the post of acting Director of Marketing for a main region of their business.

His first big challenge was to find £80K of savings from the marketing budget (annual). He had a couple of weeks to work out a plan and prepare a presentation for the Board – a Progress Report on Marketing.

The plan was no trouble. He knew exactly what he wanted to do. In fact, he believed he could save £100K annually with ease. The presentation was more of a problem. The Board, Dave informed me, had the attention span of a gnat. Interesting. No Board I had ever encountered was like that. Mostly they are composed of razor-sharp, motivated, insightful people all too capable of fixing on a subject and getting to its heart in a moment. What was going on here? Was this something to do with the Board, or actually with Dave's presentations? Was he – typically – talking for too long, or not about the right things, or in the wrong way about the right things – or something else?

I asked Dave if he had any idea of how to do the presentation.

Actually, he'd already written it. In principle, at any rate. The problem, he felt, was how to deliver it in a compelling way. What was he planning to say? He gave me the headlines. First he'd cover Marketing: how we got here. Then Marketing: where we are now. Finally, Marketing: where we are going.

Recognize it? It's a classic school essay. It's got a clear three-part structure, so beloved of English teachers. It also has a familiar speech format: past, present, future. It is focused and would, no doubt, prove that Dave had mastery of Marketing in his company. But what would the Board – his audience – experience? Marketing, how we got here. They know that – THEY'RE THE BOARD. They lived through it, and disliked it first time. That's why Dave's boss had to go. Sitting through a recap is going to be tedious at best. Marketing: where we are now. THEY KNOW THAT TOO. That's why Dave needs to make £80K of savings.

So the first two-thirds of the presentation are redundant. Assuming it is 20 minutes, the first twelve or so are sheer torture for busy, stressed executives whose budgets are under pressure. But Dave's their new guy, and this is his first presentation to them in his new position, and they don't want to knock his confidence, so they'll probably just suffer in silence. That explains his 'attention span of a gnat' comment. He has presented to them before, and previously bored them, and they were too polite to stop him.

Time for Dave to discover a different approach to preparing a presentation.

GOER®

I call my technique 'GOER'. It has four distinct stages.

GOAL	This is when you establish precisely what you want your presentation to do. In other words, the meaning of your presentation.
	If you do not know this, you will only achieve your goal – if you manage to at all – by accident. If you know it, and have been explicit about it, you stand a high chance of achieving it.
OUTLINE	You decide what you need to communicate in order to achieve your goal.
ELABORATE	You decide how to communicate what needs to be communicated.
REFINE	You take an objective view of what you have produced and make sure it works.

GOAL is covered in Chapter 2. It involves doing some work with your audience, but does not take long.

OUTLINE is covered in Chapter 3. It is surprisingly quick to do (but requires some quite lengthy explanations) and also involves interacting with your audience.

ELABORATE is the subject of Chapter 4. It is easy to do.

REFINE, the subject of Chapter 5, is longer, when you polish what you have created. But with GOER, at least you know that you are polishing something that will deliver.

Using GOER to prepare your presentations has many benefits.

- Less nerves

With GOER, you know, from an early stage, that what you are going to say will work, because you've communicated with the audience in an appropriate way from the outset. That calms most people's nerves a great deal.

- More time

GOER takes less time to implement than the School Essay Technique.

- More fun

GOER is not a solemn approach. It's quite fun to do. It uses tools and techniques that suit the way we think.

- Builds mental capacity

GOER helps you build the strength of your creativity and memory.

- More exciting

GOER rarely produces mundane presentations. It almost always enables people to produce something that is true to themselves – which means unique. That makes the whole business of preparing and doing presentations exciting.

Imagine you were really good at presentations, able to tackle them without worrying, and sure that when you did one, it stood an excellent chance of working. What would be the benefit to your work life? Those I coach who become more effective at doing presentations experience quite a lot of change, some of it surprising (covered in Chapter 8). They also experience some more obvious benefits.

1) Personal

You will become less anxious. You will achieve more workplace goals. You will, as a result, get your way more often.

That will probably result in your being more effective all round, and happier at work.

2) For your audience/co-workers/colleagues/team
You will supply more valuable, relevant information in your presentations, more clearly and quickly. Everyone who works with you will appreciate that, which will enhance your status in the workplace. The projects which you contribute to will tend to go in the right direction more often (because your presentations will be more effective), so that will also increase the respect with which you are regarded.

3) For your business
Good presentations often result in improved results for your business. Your bosses will notice that when you are in a team, and when you do presentations, projects tend to go better. That can only do you good.

4) For your career
One of the distinguishing characteristics of people who thrive in the workplace is that they can communicate what they want effectively to groups of others. Get good at presentations, and your career will benefit.

So what makes a good presenter?

A good presenter
People who attend my workshops feel a good presenter:

- Makes the information interesting and relevant to the audience.
- Is real (other words that frequently come up are: genuine, sincere, honest, truthful).
- And is NOT reciting a speech, preaching, lecturing or being patronising.

Notice, there is nothing in the description of a good presenter about being confident, humorous or witty – all those qualities that, typically, people who are nervous of doing presentations feel they lack. Those may be relevant to speeches – but striving to be so is irrelevant (or worse, counterproductive) for presentations. Primarily, audiences want you to be you. You know about your subject – that's usually why you are doing the presentation. The challenge is to communicate what you know in an engaging, authentic way. Helping you do that is a large part of what this book is about.

It is my belief that, given support and encouragement – and this book aims to supply that – you will be able to stand up in front of a group as yourself and know that this is of value to your audience. That's what they are interested in. You.

What did that mean in Dave's case?

Dave's presentation
Introduced to GOER, Dave decided his Audience Objective was to discover how he proposed to save £80K. His own aim (and I believe all presentations should have two aims: yours, and your audience's) was to establish his authority as the new Marketing Director. He also established that he wanted to communicate his plan quickly, and leave plenty of time for discussion with the Board.

The **O**utline stage didn't take long. Dave just laid out the bones of his plan. He did **E**laborate during his commute to work in his car with the radio off. By the time he reached work, he had the whole thing sorted out in his mind. Refine took a little longer, which is usual. This is the stage when the PowerPoint slides he wanted were produced, and when he prepared a set of handouts.

His presentation started along these lines.

> *'Good morning. Today I'm going to explain how I propose NOT to save £80K on our annual marketing budget, but £100K. And increase our impact.'*

He told me that from those words onwards, he had the Board's undivided attention throughout the entire 14 minutes of his presentation, and that they had a fruitful discussion afterwards. And soon after that he was made up to permanent Director of Marketing for his region.

Action Step: Select a presentation

To get the best from this book, please now select a presentation to apply the ideas to as you read. The ideal one is not so far in the future that you will not start work on it now, but not so soon that you haven't got enough time to do some experimental work. Four weeks is about right. It's also best if it is not too high-stakes, but not too irrelevant either. You don't want to do your first differently prepared presentation to your boss with your job on the line (unless that's why you picked up this book, in which case – go for it!). Equally, you don't want it to be a presentation which has little or nothing riding on it (e.g. one to your family on your hobby). Something like a regular team briefing is ideal.

Reading this book without applying it to an actual presentation is a bit like trying to learn to swim by reading a Teach Yourself Swimming book cover to cover at home, and only then going to a swimming pool. Working on a presentation as you read this book is more like having a swimming coach with you as you learn a new stroke.

Having dumped the idea of doing a presentation like a school essay, it's time to surface some hidden ideas that may be influencing the way you approach presentations.

IMPLICIT AND EXPLICIT RULES

Some rules in life are explicit. They are said out loud. A sign reading 'Do not step on the grass' is one such. Other rules are implicit. They are not said out loud, just understood. One such is that we do not pick flowers in a public park. The flowers are there for everyone to enjoy.

It is relatively easy to flout explicit rules. You see the sign, you see the expanse of lawn, you might even see, in the distance, others lounging on it. It's a hot day, and the grass is inviting. You might just flop down on it.

Implicit rules are much harder to break, partly because they seem to be part of ourselves. Even if you were to see someone picking flowers in a public park, even if you wanted flowers for your home, would you start doing it yourself? I have only once seen someone pluck a rose in a park, and they were roundly scolded by others.

We have considered some of the explicit rules governing school essays, but what are the implicit ones? Here's a list produced by participants in a workshop.

A school essay must be:

- Long enough.
- Full of information.
- About what the title says it is about.
- Formal.
- All your own work.

We've already disposed of 'long enough' and 'full of information'. That leaves titles, formality and your own work.

Titles

A truth of the school essay is that, if it is not written about the title, it will get no marks. If the title is 'My Holidays', it's no good writing about your family, even if what you produce is wonderful. Workplace presentations are not quite like that. If the title is 'A Progress Report on Marketing' that does NOT mean you have to produce just that. In the workplace, the title is just shorthand for describing your presentation. The Board did not hassle Dave because he did not follow the exact meaning of the title. Quite the reverse: they were delighted with his going behind and beyond the title.

Formality

Must a presentation be formal? For what reason should you, when updating your peers on something you know about, be anything other than your normal, informal self? So forget about standing to deliver your presentation – unless that is something you feel comfortable doing. Present yourself as you are. That's much preferable to becoming an awkward school kid, politely shuffling around in front of the adults.

All your own work

This is the most toxic, and least relevant, of the implicit rules governing a school essay. What is not working alone called in school? Cheating. It is strongly discouraged and severely punished. But in today's workplace that attitude is completely inappropriate. After all, we're all being constantly urged to be better team players, to collaborate, dialogue, share and consult. So forget about preparing your presentation alone. Embrace the power of collaborative working.

SUMMARY

A presentation is not a speech. It is much easier than that. It is not about writing and then reading out an essay. It is much easier than that. It is simply about communicating something you know well to your audience in an effective way.

To see how to do that, read on.

Andy was an ambitious young company lawyer, a star in the making. He hired me to help him get to the next level – a seat on a company's Board. He'd seen a job advertisement for Legal Director of a small concern, applied and got an interview. He was short-listed and, as one of the final three in contention for the post, was told he'd now have to do a presentation to the CEO. I asked Andy about what he proposed to present and he was relaxed. He was going to tell the CEO about his education, qualifications and experience.

Recognize that? Once again, it's the School Essay Technique rearing its ugly head. What's the problem with what he was planning to say? Think of it from the point of view of his audience – the CEO. It was, presumably, precisely on account of his education, qualifications and so on that Andy got the interview. Reciting this material would be boring – hardly the best impression to make in an interview – and would be wasting a valuable opportunity to influence the CEO before Andy (hopefully) got offered the job.

So, what did the CEO actually want from Andy's presentation? In terms of GOER, this is always the most important question when considering **G**oal.

THE REASON THE AUDIENCE OBJECTIVE IS VITAL

The reason it helps if you are explicit with yourself about the Audience Objective at the outset of using GOER is that, unless you know what they are interested in, you are only going to satisfy them, if you do so at all, by chance. And if you don't deliver on what they want, your presentation is not going to be successful. But it's also because by asking yourself (and them) this question in a serious and respectful way at the outset, you put yourself into listening, rather than talking, mode.

That might seem strange, given that you are doing a presentation, but think about it. Who is more attractive to you: someone you find interesting, or someone who finds you interesting? Someone you find interesting is often attractive at first. But if they go on being interesting, and that's it, their attractiveness begins to wane. It's like they're doing a song-and-dance act. It's fine for a while, but then gets boring. However, if someone finds you interesting, that is a connection, and a valuable dialogue can develop out of it.

It's like that with presentations. If you approach it from the point of view of being interesting to the audience, you'll become little more than someone doing an act. If, however, your audience sense that you are interested in them, you are on your way to establishing a bond between you.

Also, attitudes are contagious. When you meet someone friendly and open, how do you feel towards them? Most of us tend to feel friendly too. When you meet someone hostile, how do you feel towards them? Again, hostility is rewarded with hostility. When preparing a presentation, if you do it from the attitude that you have listened to the audience, they will sense that, and will respond in kind, by listening to you.

It is worth examining for a moment what an audience in a presentation feel.

HOW DO AN AUDIENCE FEEL?

The surest way to know this is to consider how you feel when you go into a meeting and you realize someone is about to do a presentation. Do you mentally prepare your nought to ten score cards, ready to judge their performance? Or does the thought flit across your mind: I hope this is good, and delivers worthwhile information in a useful way? That's what I feel, and what I believe most of us feel. We – the audience – are your allies, on your side, friendly, willing you to do well. As long as you have done your preparation, and deliver on what we want from your presentation, we'll support you enthusiastically.

So what is the best way of discovering what your audience want from your presentation? It's easy. You just talk to them.

DISCOVERING THE AUDIENCE OBJECTIVE

There are two magic questions to use in this initial conversation with your audience:

1. What would you love to hear me talk about?
2. What would you hate to hear me talk about?

What are the benefits of asking these questions? The most obvious is that you'll find out for sure what your audience are, and aren't, interested in. Once you know this, you can present them with what they'd love to hear, and avoid talking about what they wouldn't. In one step, you've eliminated many of the problems associated with presentations.

Next is that you begin your relationship with your audience way before the presentation itself. If, at the presentation, you deliver on what they told you they wanted to hear, you back up any message about the level of service you offer with a demonstration of it. Very powerful.

In terms of sales, too, this is a contact with your audience. It is a salesman's mantra that it takes six (seven? five?) 'touches' to sell anything to a customer. What that means is that for you to sell anything, a customer has to have encountered you a number of times. Each time you 'touch' them, you get nearer the magic number that they require to buy. This research gives you one of those precious 'touches'.

This conversation will give you other vital information. It will expose you to how your audience talk, think, the level of technical vocabulary they use, what they currently know about, and what they don't. That enables you to deliver your message much more accurately in your presentation.

OBJECTION TO AUDIENCE RESEARCH

Occasionally a coachee will protest that the audience will object to this call. Aren't you the presenter? Shouldn't you know what to say? That misses the point. You are making this call precisely because you have lots to say on the subject – but only want to present what the audience will find most useful. Five minutes of dialogue now will establish this, and enable you to make the presentation – and any meeting that follows – as productive as possible.

On a practical note, I'm often asked how many members of the audience you need to talk to. Three is more than enough. That's because an audience is a special collection of people.

AN AUDIENCE

Something links each person in the audience to each other. They are not there at random, because they had nothing better to do with their time. In a workplace presentation, your audience will have some specialist knowledge that relates to something to do with the subject you are presenting on.

Visually, this can be represented thus:

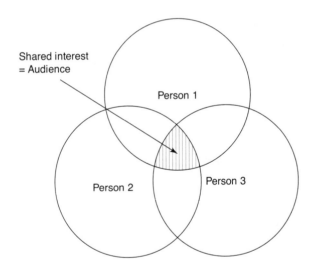

Speak to one member of the audience, and you'll hear their personal interest, plus the shared interest, but you won't necessarily know which is which. Speak to two, and you'll hear the shared interest come into focus. By the time you speak to three, the shared interest will be crystal clear. Speak to that shared interest in your presentation and you'll be speaking to the whole audience.

That said, as you become more familiar with using GOER, you'll be increasingly able to talk to just one member of the audience to get this information. The trick is to listen in the right way, to the meaning level.

GUIDE TO LISTENING AT THE MEANING LEVEL

Listening at the meaning level is not a passive activity. It is not just allowing the words to fall on your ears. To do it involves, amongst other things, listening:

- To the tone, pace and emotions when people talk. In the example in Chapter 1, Dolores seemed to respond immediately, without checking her diary. How many of us truly know what we're doing a fortnight and a month from now? If Brad is paying attention, that tells him something.
- For links and patterns in what people say. Is Dolores apparently struggling to find a date to meet Brad, or rather seeking to find ways not to meet?
- To what people do NOT say. For example, Dolores did not suggest a time when she and Brad might meet.

Listening in this way involves really attending to what the other person says. Try to resist the temptation to jump to conclusions, but instead ask lots of interested questions.

Stretch: Listening to meaning
Over the next few days, experiment with listening to what people mean as well as what they say. Note what it does to the quality of your conversations.

AUDIENCE RESEARCH

Back to GOER. When you talk to your audience about what they'd love to hear you talk about, and hate to hear you talk about, listen on the meaning level. Seek to get into dialogue with them about what they say. You might ask them about their reasons for wanting you to do a particular sort of presentation. Is a presentation what they really want from you, or would they prefer something else – something more interactive? How much of a chance do they want to question you? Do they want more detail, or more of an overview, or both? What sort of handouts might help?

As you listen to their answers, you may immediately get ideas about what your presentation might be like. Share them with the person you are talking to and listen carefully to what they say. Do they really like it, or are they being enthusiastic merely to finish the conversation, or to make you feel good? Ask them for their ideas, and listen intently.

I stress this because people rarely express what they mean without some encouragement. Remember, Dolores *never actually says her meaning*. This is quite common. In the real world, most of us assume the other person will 'get' what we mean. This has profound implications for presentations (and for life and communications in general; but more of that later).

In some situations, however, it is not that straightforward to just 'talk to the audience'. Take Andy, for instance. He can hardly call the CEO who is going to interview him and ask the magic questions. What can he do?

RESEARCH WHEN YOU CAN'T
TALK TO THE AUDIENCE

If, like Andy, you cannot talk to the audience, do your research with someone who can model their minds. That means someone who knows how they think, and can think like that themselves. In Andy's case, it turned out to be surprisingly easy to find such a person. His godfather had been a CEO, so Andy called him, described the situation and asked the magic questions. The answers he got were invaluable.

His godfather told him that, as CEO, he would want a potential candidate for the post of Legal Director to talk about the legal challenges facing the company and their proposals for dealing with them. And nothing else. That's because, as CEO, his godfather was always under intense time pressure. He would have been looking for someone who understood that, and could cut straight to the legal heart of any issue. Andy was delighted. He could easily do *that* presentation.

A warning here. Do not short-cut this research by talking to someone who just deals with your audience, but isn't one of them themselves. Sarah made this mistake. An expert on work–life balance, she'd had feedback that her presentations were not strong. We started work on a presentation she was going to do to Scottish doctors. She'd done several on the same subject to English doctors and was very reluctant to do audience research. Scottish doctors, she believed, were just like English ones, only with a different accent. She wanted me to advise her on hand gestures, breathing and the like.

Now, I'm a coach, and it's my job to support those I coach to thrive, and in this case I felt she needed to check her assumptions. So I persisted in asking her to do the research. At our next coaching session, Sarah had a triumphant look on her face. Had she done her research? Yes. Was it revealing? No. That was interesting. What had she discovered? She'd discovered that she was right. Scottish doctors are just like English ones: demanding, disorganized, self-centred, with no common sense. What do you notice about that description?

What I noticed is that it is unlike a description a person would use about themselves, or their peer group. I was intrigued – who had she actually talked to? The organizer of the conference, a woman whose job it was to make sure the event went well. Do you see what Sarah had got? She had not got the thoughts of a Scottish doctor, or someone who could model their minds. She had heard the prejudices of someone who had to deal with them. That's worse than useless. (Just imagine, for a moment, the disastrous presentation the contempt in her attitude would produce.)

I persisted in asking her to speak to a Scottish doctor. I was sure she could do it easily given her huge network of contacts. At which point, she suddenly brightened. Her brother-in-law was a Scottish surgeon – close enough to a doctor – and an ideal person to talk to. All she had to do was phone her sister to get his work number. Two calls. Next session I could immediately see that Sarah had made a shift. Had she done the research? Yes. Had it been useful? Absolutely.

What Sarah had discovered is that, unknown to her, the Scottish parliament had just published a White Paper on work–life balance in the NHS in Scotland. Imagine she had not discovered that and had gone to Scotland and done her standard presentation. Even with the benefit of deep breathing and powerful hand gestures, as soon as her audience, all of whom presumably knew about the White Paper, realized she didn't – and they'd have spotted that near the beginning when she didn't mention it – they'd have felt she was just another stuck-up English so-called expert who had not bothered to do their homework and come to Scotland to pontificate at them. It could have been an uncomfortable experience for her.

SIX DEGREES OF SEPARATION

An aside on Sarah and Andy's research. They found someone to talk to by using their networks. If you can't speak to the audience directly, your network is the resource that will provide all you need. If it is not an immediate contact, a contact of a contact, or the contact of a contact of a contact, will get you what you want. By asking your contacts for an introduction to someone you are looking for, you can reach almost anyone in the business world. This is doubly true if you are not looking for a particular person but instead for someone who fits a generic description, i.e. a Project Manager, or an academic who commissions training, or whatever. In fact, it has been established that it takes only six jumps to reach virtually anyone in the developed world. This idea is called 'six degrees of separation' – Google it if you want to know more.

Note!
Later in the GOER process, at the **O**utline stage, you will make another short call. These people you have initially spoken to are the ideal ones to speak to again. So, during this initial conversation, ask them permission for you to call them back later for just 5 minutes.

Action Step: Speak to the audience
Select three members of the audience for the presentation you are applying GOER to and have a conversation with them about what they'd love to hear you talk about, and what they'd hate to hear you talk about.

Listen for their imagery, the attitudes they share, their vocabulary, their level of expertise, the pacing of the way they communicate information.

You might – if you feel brave – ask them to co-create the presentation with you. Brainstorm with the first person you talk to what the presentation might be like. Then use these ideas to brainstorm further with the second. By the time you do the third call, you will have quite detailed ideas that they will be responding enthusiastically to. Remember to end the call by asking their permission to make a second, short call sometime later.

Laura, a banker who hated doing presentations, objected to doing this work the first time we talked about it. She said that, as a senior figure in the financial world, she couldn't go around asking people what they wanted to hear from her. The presentation in question was for a regular, monthly meeting of the many major institutions which were stakeholders in her company. It was the first time she was doing this presentation which had, in the past, been done by the company's MD.

In spite of her reservations, Laura made the three calls, just as an experiment. She discovered that the stakeholders were dissatisfied with the way these meetings had been done in the past. Instead of the 45-minute lecture they usually suffered, what they really wanted to hear was what other stakeholders felt about the way the company was operating. Laura was delighted to discover this. Instead of having to slave over a lengthy presentation, all she had to do was turn up, greet everyone and chair a sharing session. Being immensely courageous, that was precisely what she did. To begin the meeting, she introduced herself, explained that she wanted to hear from each person in the room – there were twenty of them – and then kept quiet. The hour was, apparently, an astounding success. Afterwards, several of those attending emailed her to say it was the best such meeting they'd had, and could it become the default format in the future?

She then said these classic words to me: 'The question for me now is not "why should I contact my audience before a presentation?", it's why would I ever *not* do it?' That's my personal standard too. I will not walk into a room to do a communication I have had time to prepare without first having talked to the audience (or someone who can model their mind). NEVER. It's as simple as that.

CREATING AN AUDIENCE OBJECTIVE

Once you've done this research, sum up what you feel the Audience Objective is in one sentence. Keep it short and sweet. It usually starts with the word 'To'.

Andy decided his audience, the CEO, simply wanted:

> '*To understand if you are the right person for this job.*'

Sarah decided doctors in Scotland wanted her:

> '*To explain how to improve the work–life balance of Scottish doctors in the NHS.*'

Laura's audience wanted:

> '*To know what other stakeholders felt about the way the company was going.*'

Ideally, an Audience Objective is muscular. This would not be a useful formulation for Andy:

> *'To understand how you see the legal position of our compa-*
> *ny and explain how you aim to tackle it and how you would*
> *do it better than anyone else and (deep breath) how you are*
> *the best person for the job of Legal Director.'*

That's not an objective, it's a shopping list. It would produce an unfocused, sprawling presentation. So spend a little time getting the formulation of the Audience Objective taut. It will be at the heart of your presentation from now on, the touchstone you can turn to when you are deep in the process and suddenly remember that fantastic anecdote about the time the Regional Office put the wrong figure in the spreadsheet and that meant . . . at which point you can turn back to your Audience Objective and ask: 'Is this relevant?' If it is, it's in. If not, it's out.

Action Step: Craft an Audience Objective
Craft a single sentence that sums up your Audience Objective. Ensure it is simple. You will recognize it when you find it because you are likely to get a thrill of recognition, one that says 'That's it!'

Simple versus simplistic
The best Audience Objectives are simple. Simple, but not simplistic. Simplistic is when simple has been dumbed down. Simple is getting to the essence of a communication, and expressing it clearly. Simple is powerful, and – actually – not that easy to do. But worth striving for.

The trick is to do it over a period of time. Come up with a formulation and step away from it. Come back to it and listen to what you have decided. Does it give you a thrill that says: 'Yes, that's it!' If not, come up with something different. Step away from it – do another task – and return. Is the thrill there? If not, try again, or divert your mind to something else absorbing. Trust that the answer will come.

Stretch: Developing a simple style
Tune your mind to notice strong, simple communications.
Advertisements on television often have wonderfully simple scripts and
slogans. Notice the ones that work, and those that do not.

Experiment with writing simple emails. Simple, clear and complete.

You have already completed the most time-consuming part of the **G**oal stage of GOER. We're now going to go through a number of questions to ask yourself to complete **G**oal. The form below sums them up.

Title of Presentation:	
Audience Objective	
Your Intention	
Action at End?	
Duration	
Deadlines:	
• First Draft • Slides? • Handouts? • Final Approval • Delivery	
Final Approval	
Support	

You may find it useful to photocopy it and fill it in as you use the GOER process. We've gone through the first line, Audience Objective. Time to look at Your Intention.

YOUR INTENTION

I was talking informally to Beth, an in-house multimedia producer I had worked with when I was a scriptwriter. For those unfamiliar with 'multimedias', they were a hybrid of corporate video and computer training. They were expensive to make and hell to produce as they combined all the difficulty of filming, with the nightmare that is IT. She was preparing a presentation for a conference of multimedia producers.

Out of curiosity, I asked the reason she was doing it. She was doing it because she had been invited to. Intrigued, I asked why she had accepted. Because a lot of in-house producers and commissioners of multimedias would be there. Duh. That really confused me. Beth had a job I thought she enjoyed, in a major corporation, with superb perks and staff support systems and – as far as I knew – got on well with everyone she worked with. So why was it significant that the audience were in-house producers and commissioners?

A cunning look crossed her face, she shot a glance over her shoulder to check no-one could overhear, then leant in to me. 'Because I'm pregnant.' Now seriously confused, I (quietly) congratulated her, and asked the inescapable question. What did her being pregnant have to do with the presentation? 'Because I plan to go freelance after my maternity leave and the audience are my potential clients.'

Bingo. We had established what I call 'Your Intention' – the reason she was doing the presentation. Because note this: there are *always* two aims, two objectives to a presentation. One is the audience's, the other is yours. Fail to deliver on both, simultaneously, and the presentation won't really work. Deliver on both, and you – and the audience – will be satisfied.

Imagine Beth's presentation without our having surfaced her intention. It might go something like this:

> *'Hi, I'm Beth, the in-house multimedia producer for XYZ Corporation.'*

> *'Now, we all know that multimedias are difficult to produce.'*

(Audience all nod)

> *'They are time-consuming, expensive and complex to get right.'*

(More nods)

> *'And if they go wrong, whose head is it on the block?'*

(Pained silence)

> *'Ours – the in-house producers.'*

(She has the audience in the palm of her hands).

> *'To help ensure my multimedias NEVER go wrong, I've developed a 42-stage process that is foolproof.'*

Up comes a slide with Beth's 42 stages written on it. She turns to the screen, draws a deep breath and starts to read:

> *'Stage 1 . . . '*

(A few of the audience get out pens and paper, the rest start to bang their heads rhythmically on the nearest hard surface in an attempt to put themselves out of their misery).

Now imagine the same material, only this time she has surfaced her intention, and it is driving her presentation. The start is the same: she hooks her audience in with the idea that if a production goes wrong, they are in deep do-do. She then mentions her 42-stage process, which is guaranteed to deliver a successful multimedia. But now she says this:

> *'And, if you'd like to know more about this, I'll happily talk to you about it after the presentation, or you can email me.'*

The rest of her presentation can be about – whatever. Perhaps war stories of productions which – given Beth's immense experience of the subject – would surely deliver significant value and entertainment. At the end of this second presentation, what will happen?

Most of the audience will leave, happy to have been entertained and with some nuggets of useful information. But some, those most urgently in need of help with their multimedia productions, will stay to talk to her. After all, she has just proved herself to be both entertaining and experienced. They are warm prospects. And some, those most in need of support, will contact her by email for the 42-step process. They are hot prospects. Job done, both for them, and for herself.

The fact that presentations always have two objectives is one of the many reasons they are so hard to do well, and – again – why the School Essay Technique is so ill-suited to preparing one. In a few situations you will know instinctively what Your Intention is. In others, it will take some delving to uncover. Personally, I use a tool called the 'Five Whys' to do that.

THE FIVE WHYS

The 'Five Whys' was originally, I believe, used in engineering to uncover the cause of a problem and not just the symptoms (Google to discover more). It consists of using a series of questions beginning with the word 'Why' to drive an enquiry deeper. I was using the Five Whys above in my dialogue with Beth.

In principle, you construct the questions by taking the answer to the question before and attaching a 'Why' to it. You occasionally use a different questioning word, but mostly it's just 'why'. Used properly – and it does require some skill and practice – it will give you an answer that expresses the meaning of your presentation. Personally, I often use the Five Whys before major meetings, before responding to important emails, before crucial phone calls. It helps me to communicate across the board with a greatly heightened awareness of what I want, which enables me to get more results, more of the time.

Here's another example of how it works. What might Andy's intention have been for his presentation? The obvious answer is:

'To get the job as Legal Director of the company.'

Now let's apply the Five Whys to it. Let's imagine doing it with Andy (which, in truth, we did).

Why do you want the job?

'Because I want to become the Legal Director of a company.'

Why do you want to become Legal Director of a company?

'Because the next step in my career is to sit on a company's Board and make the big decisions.'

Why does getting this job enable you to sit on the company's Board?

'Er, it doesn't. At least, not necessarily.'

That was significant. The Five Whys had focused Andy's attention on the fact that the advertisement did not actually specify that the Legal Director sat on the Board. He was just hoping that if he got offered the job, he could ask for a seat on the Board. By working on his intention, it had become clear that his presentation should not be simply about getting the job, it should be about getting the job *as long as it came with a seat on the Board.*

As it relates to presentations, the Five Whys leads you from the hearing level of content – what you are going to say to satisfy the Audience Objective – to the meaning level, which is Your Intention.

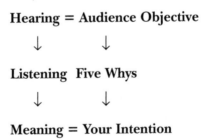

Hearing = Audience Objective

↓   ↓

Listening Five Whys

↓   ↓

Meaning = Your Intention

Once you have both the Audience Objective and Your Intention, you know what your presentation has to do.

HOW TO CONSTRUCT YOUR INTENTION

Your Intention, like the Audience Objective, is best expressed by one, simple, strong sentence with no frills. In Beth's case, it might have been:

'To make contact with potential employers for when I go freelance.'

And Sarah's intention, with her Scottish doctors? As soon as I asked her, she replied that it was to win some work for her organization. Why would the presentation win her this work? Because they would see she was insightful and real-world, not a head-in-the-clouds academic. Once again, Sarah surfacing her intention fed into the meaning of her presentation.

Action Step: Craft Your Intention
Formulate Your Intention.

If you are interested, experiment with the Five Whys. Starting with your formulation of the Audience Objective, use the Five Whys to construct a neat sentence which expresses Your Intention. You may have to do it several times, varying the questions. If you discover that you are going round in circles ('To get a seat on the Board', Why do you want a seat on the Board?, 'Because I want a seat on the Board') you have got an answer, although possibly not The Answer. Vary the questions and see if you come up with the same thing, or with something else. Listen to all the replies, and seek to learn from all of them. If you do not come up with a useful answer, is this presentation really necessary?

You will know when you have got to the truth of Your Intention because it will feel energized when you say it.

Although it has taken quite a few pages to get this far, how long will it take in the real world to do these two key activities?

Audience Objective: a few phone calls and a couple of fairly short conversations – 20 minutes, half an hour tops?

Your Intention: a couple of turns through the Five Whys. Five minutes?

And these two ideas will provide your presentation with a rock solid foundation.

Stretch
Use the Five Whys regularly. Become skilled with it. Notice the difference it makes when you go into an interaction with a powerful intention, compared to when you go in not having prepared in this way.

Goal, in terms of GOER, is nearly complete. We've just got a couple more things to sort out, starting with Action at End.

ACTION AT END

A friend of mine told me that, as a teenager, he experimented with a seduction technique from a joke. The joke is that a man asks a woman at a party if she wants to go upstairs and have sex with him immediately after they've been introduced. Affronted, she slaps his face. 'I bet you get a lot of slaps doing that', she storms. 'I do', he replies. 'And I get a lot of sex too.' My friend, still grinning after all these years, confided that an astounding number of girls, when asked straight out, did in fact say yes to the proposition.

So consider whether or not you want to ask the audience to do something at the end of your presentation. Of course, not every presentation has to have an Action at End; plenty of them are for other purposes. But research has established that people underestimate the likelihood of the other party saying 'yes', so they often just don't ask because they assume the answer is going to be no. If you are pitching for a contract, it's worth, at the end of your presentation, saying something as basic as 'I hope we get the contract'.

After all, like my friend with his seduction technique, if you don't ask, you won't get. Which brings us to duration.

DURATION

Andy's job interview was an hour. How long should his presentation be? Many people think at least 20 minutes. Let's examine that.

Say the interview is scheduled from 10.00 to 11.00:

10.00	11.00

When does the interview start? One thing is virtually guaranteed. NOT at 10.00. Even in the best run organizations, it's going to be 10.05 at the earliest. And then there's some time to be spent Making Nice ('Good journey? Did you find us all right?'), there's hospitality, plus a quick comfort break.

So what is a realistic time the interview starts? How about 10.15?

10.00 10.15	11.00

That leaves 45 minutes. Plenty of time for a 20-minute presentation.

And when does the mind of the main decision-maker leave this meeting? Because, after this meeting, the CEO will have something else to do, something fun, like balancing budgets, or restructuring a department that isn't working, or outsourcing some jobs. It's realistic to imagine that sometime before the end, the CEO's mind will go to this next task. How about we say 15 minutes?

10.00 10.15   10.45 11.00

30 minutes of functional meeting left – just enough for a 20-minute presentation.

And what value should Andy place on questions and answers versus his presentation? When I first asked him this question, he said: Presentation 70%, Q&As 30%.

Let's think about that for a moment. What happens if someone leaves your presentation with a question in their mind which you haven't had time to answer? What are they going to be thinking about? Your presentation, or their unanswered question? Almost everyone will focus on their unanswered question – which will reduce the value of your presentation to zero.

So, what value now on presentation versus Q&A? Before we decide on that, notice something else. In many presentations there's a third element – experience of what you are saying. Imagine, for instance, that I'm doing a presentation on coaching. What will the audience want? First, for me to talk about coaching. Second, to have time to ask questions.

And, third, perhaps, to see what coaching looks like. In fact, many coaches have discovered that the vital element when doing a presentation about coaching is to demonstrate it. Think of a sales pitch for a product. Talking about the product is fine, but nothing replaces actually experiencing it.

So did Andy want an element of 'experience' in his presentation? This question focused him on the fact that, in his position, Q&As are precisely 'experience' for his prospective employer. After all, a CEO wants a lawyer who can handle tough questions, argue and negotiate his case.

Looked at that way, Andy decided to reverse the split: Presentation 30%, Q&As 70%. 30% of 30 minutes is 9 minutes. So what would have happened if Andy had gone into the interview with a 20-minute presentation?

Imagine the CEO is relatively prompt, turning up at 10.07. He apologizes for being late, and disappears again to get a coffee. He's not back till 10.13. There's a bit of sociable chit-chat. They discover a common interest and have a laugh together. Unfortunately for Andy, time is slipping by. Now he's in a dilemma. He knows it's important that he and the CEO get on, but the presentation has to start soon or there'll not be enough time for it. So at 10.30 Andy engineers a stop to the chit-chat in order to launch into his presentation. He feels, instinctively, that the CEO didn't really appreciate this, but hey, needs must. At 10.45 Andy catches the CEO glancing at his watch . . . got to hurry! What to do now? Gabble? Miss a chunk? Omit the end?

I've sat through innumerable presentations where the presenters have taken each of these options, and sometimes all of them. You must have too. And isn't it unimpressive?

Personally, I particularly hate it when, after suffering through endless slides of unendurable complexity, of having the presenter read them to me slowly – I do that reading thing quite well myself, it's a trick I picked up at school – they realize that time is running out and announce that we're now going to start skipping slides. Does this mean the earlier slides were optional too? If so, couldn't we have skipped a whole bunch from the beginning and saved ourselves the tedium of sitting through them?

What actually happened when Andy turned up for his interview was that the CEO wasn't there at all. His PA explained that there had been a crisis over the weekend in India and the CEO was in Bangalore. The interview would be via video link. It started at just past 10.00, but the technology immediately crashed. The link was finally working again at 10.30. The CEO was apologetic – but Andy was cool. Fifteen love to Andy.

Andy did his presentation calmly, frightening the bejabbers out of the exhausted CEO with his assessment of the legal challenges facing the company. Thirty love. Andy then outlined how, in order to deal adequately with these challenges, he would require a seat on the Board. Forty love. The CEO pushed back on the salary Andy was asking for and they agreed a deal (Andy had already decided he wasn't too bothered about the salary – it was the position he wanted). Game, set and match to Andy.

People frequently ask what happens if, against all precedent, a meeting starts on time and you've only prepared a short presentation? You have two choices. The first is to talk more, add an extra example, embroider a story. This is relatively straightforward to do. At REFINE stage of GOER you will have taken out quite a lot of material. Now's the opportunity to slip some of it back in. The second: do the short presentation, leaving more time for questions. After all, have you ever heard a workplace audience leaving a presentation saying 'Damn, I wish that presentation had been longer!' I never have. People LOVE short presentations that do the business.

There is another reason you should always plan to talk less. That is because of the value you will be expected to deliver.

VALUE AND DURATION

Even if the people attending your presentation are in the same offices as yours, they will have to expend a significant amount of time in order to attend. Five minutes to leave their desk, 5 minutes to establish themselves in the new location, and the same to return to their desks at the end. Twenty minutes of unproductive time. Obviously, if they come from further, it's more.

When you now take up their time by talking at them, i.e. presenting as it is all-too-often done, they expect that to be worth listening to. Not just on a one-to-one basis, but to make up for the time and trouble getting there. So, for instance, if you are talking for 20 minutes, something inside of them is saying – is this worth it? It's almost like going out to eat. Because you are taking the trouble to leave your home, you want the meal to be better than normal. If your presentation is not an extra worthwhile way of spending their time, they will begrudge you wasting their lives.

So the onus is on you to (a) talk only as long as you need to and (b) provide great value when you do. After all, a presentation is a communication you have had time to prepare in advance. The audience expect you to have used your time making sure they don't waste theirs.

Action Step: Decide on the duration

Think about the duration of your presentation, taking into account when it is likely to start; when the minds of those in the meeting will drift on to their next obligation; and the value you place on the presentation itself, Q&As and the chance for the audience to experience what you are talking about (if appropriate).

Deadlines:

- First Draft
- Slides?
- Handouts?
- Final Approval
- Delivery

The School Essay Technique fools us into thinking that the deadline for our presentation is the date of delivery. That is absurd. Let's suppose you were due to do an important presentation. The line below represents the time from now, till then:

Now   Date of Presentation

Let's suppose also that you want to present the client with some diagrams and photographs, so you decide that you're going to need PowerPoint slides. How long will it take to prepare them? Remember, you've got to get all the images right, and fiddle with the wording and layout. How long do you want to schedule for that? *Note:* we are not thinking now of cramming all the work into a day, we're thinking of an ideal world where you do an hour here, an hour there – returning to the work frequently to view it as an outsider and so spot mistakes.

Let's indicate that time graphically with a block:

Now   Date of Presentation
                                       Slides

Will you want some handouts too? Something your client can make notes on, take away from the presentation, and perhaps show their team back in their office? How long will it take to get handouts right? Will you do this while you are doing your PowerPoint slides, or after? Personally, I find that the handouts are the last thing I get right. And that they come after I've sorted out the slides.

Now   Date of Presentation
                                       Handouts
                                       Slides

And I also find that Murphy's Law operates powerfully around the time I'm working on the handouts and slides. The printer cartridge runs out in the middle of the print run, and there isn't a replacement in the building, and the local stationery stores have run out of that cartridge at the moment I most want it. So let's factor that in too:

Now   Date of Presentation
                                       Handouts
                                       Murphy
                                       Slides

With an important presentation, bosses mostly want to approve what you are going to say. Does your boss operate an overnight turn-around service? Most don't. And most want to glance at the whole thing: slides, handouts and all. So let's add some time for that too:

Now	Date of Presentation
	Final Approval
	Handouts
	Murphy
	Slides

How long would you like to spend deciding what you are going to say, assessing it, sharing it with your nearest and dearest, amending, going to your team, rewriting and so on? This creative work is called ELABORATE in the GOER process, so let's add it in.

Now	Date of Presentation
	Final Approval
	Handouts
	Murphy
	Slides
	Elaborate

And then there's this research I'm talking about. Got to factor that in too:

Now	Date of Presentation
	Final Approval
	Handouts
	Murphy
	Slides
	Elaborate
	Research

And we haven't even left time for your boss to see your slides and make some changes, and for you to implement those – and for your boss to see your handouts, and make some more changes . . .

What this highlights is that, in order to get a presentation done well, and for it not to dominate the days just before delivery, it's best to think about a series of key dates, rather than one final deadline. In other words, construct a critical path for yourself, marking in the dates you want to hit.

Working back from the date of delivery, decide a date you want to start work on the handouts, the slides, when you plan to get it to your boss for final approval (and book time in with them so the date is set), add a margin for Murphy in those last stages, and then some time for creative work on the presentation itself. That way, you'll have a fighting chance of getting the presentation to a mature state prior to delivery. Truth is, even with careful planning, it'll *still* be a rush at the last minute. But the work you produce will be excellent and professional, not a school kid's hurried homework.

Note, we are not talking here about the time it will take for you to work on the presentation itself. That may not be many hours. But, this way, it'll be spread across a significant period, and so will be done well.

Of course, sometimes there isn't a long run-up before a presentation. GOER works in that situation too – in fact, that's when GOER is particularly useful. But we'll examine that later (in Chapter 7: In an Emergency).

Action Step: Decide your deadlines
Decide the dates you want to start work on the slides (if any), the handouts (ditto), when you want to get this material to your boss for approval (if appropriate) and book that date with your boss, decide when you want to start the creative work and when you want to start the research.

INITIAL APPROVAL

At what stage should you seek approval for a presentation from your boss (assuming that, in your current role, you have a boss who will want to approve your presentation)? The School Essay Technique prompts us to get work polished and finished before we deliver it to teacher for marking. That's why our instinct is to present the boss with a final presentation, ready to go, for their OK and a pat on the head. But, now you've dumped the School Essay Technique, what's the smart thing to do?

Let's imagine you've done your audience research. Let's imagine too that you've discovered that your audience hate the standard, 45-minute, PowerPoint-slide-heavy presentation that is traditionally done in these meetings. They tell you that what they'd most value is a quick summary of where the project is at the moment, and then to be able to share what they're thinking with everyone else in the meeting. They're delighted that you've promised to do that.

Imagine too going to your boss just before the meeting and triumphantly presenting her with four slides: a greeting, two summing up the current situation, and a final one posing some thought-provoking questions. Remember, she's expecting a polished slide show with at least 40 slides, complete with graphs and charts, testimonials and quotations and (of course) your Mission Statement. Got to have the Mission Statement. And you are showing her four slides.

See it from her point of view. You clearly haven't done the work. Your explanation about research is nothing more than an excuse. What's the likely outcome at this point? Isn't it a stern demand that you put some work into it NOW, and come up with at least 45 minutes of dense, fact-packed, well-researched presentation supported by a minimum of 40 slides? And, if the presentation bombs − and it will, given what you've discovered about the audience − won't she just ascribe that to the fact that you left your preparation work to the last minute?

That's why it's worth going to your boss at the outset, after you've done your audience research and surfaced Your Intention. You can now present your thinking before you've invested too much work in the presentation. You can explain that you've had a conversation with the audience and what you've discovered. If your research has been done authentically, it'll make sense to your boss, as will the plan you've come up with. Your boss and you can now have a productive discussion about what you're going to do. My experience is that, approached in this way, bosses can add value at this stage. They often have a strategic and political overview that adds depth to your proposal. They can point you to people and sources of information, topics to include or avoid.

And once they've done this, what is likely to happen when, towards the end of your preparation, you come back to them with a worked-up presentation, slides and handouts? Aren't they likely to (a) understand what you are doing, (b) make constructive suggestions and (c) give you approval?

Action Step: Approval
Decide when you are first going to talk to your boss about your approach to the presentation.

SUPPORT

Who in your network can support you in creating your presentation? Someone may be able to provide expert technical advice. Someone else may be able to assist with visuals. You might know someone whom you can work with creatively. You may identify an ideal brainstorming partner. If you share this book with others (see Final Thought), you might help each other with the Five Whys and other tools. It's also immensely valuable to have a disinterested party who can give feedback on your first rehearsals.

Action Step: Identify your support

Think about who could support you in the creation of this presentation. Consider offering them this chapter to read. Using GOER is easier if you work with someone else who understands these ideas and isn't themselves fixated on the idea that a good presentation is long, stuffed with facts and aims to show how clever they are.

In the long run, it is far better to work with allies and improve what you do before the day, than discover, on it, that there are flaws which you could easily have addressed.

SUMMARY

And that concludes the **G**oal stage of GOER. How long will this whole exercise take you if you do it from scratch next time without having to refer to the book?

Audience Objective: 20 minutes? Your Intention: 5 minutes? Duration and deadlines: less than 5 minutes? Then a chat with your boss to get buy-in: 10 minutes? All done in less than an hour. And you are already way ahead of the game in terms of preparing and doing your presentation.

We're now ready to move on to the next stage in GOER, **O**utline.

I was asked to help Mike and David do a presentation in order to support the Initial Public Offering (IPO) of their conservatory construction company, Clearlight. An IPO is when a company first offers shares in itself on a public exchange. To ensure the launch goes well, it's common practice for the CEO of the company (in this case, Mike) and sometimes other senior management – in this case, David the Chief Financial Officer – to do presentations to as many major potential investors as possible. These include large financial institutions like banks, pension funds, etc.

Mike and David told me about Clearlight. They had a large factory, a considerable workforce and a turnover in the millions. We did the **G**oal stage of GOER. After some research, they were able to construct a clear and simple Audience Objective: 'To persuade the audience that theirs was a super company'. Their Intention was equally simple: 'To motivate the audience to invest in us'. To Mike and David, the word 'us' was vital: it expressed that potential investors were putting money into a management team and workforce united to build this company.

Time to move to **O**utline, the subject of this chapter. What you are aiming to generate here is four, at most five, subjects that – when presented to your audience – will deliver on their objective, and on your intention.

FOUR OR FIVE IDEAS

In the School Essay Technique we're often told – ordered – to stick to three ideas, as if there's some magic to that number. We might even have been hit over the head by some communication 'expert' with some 'research' that proves the human brain can only hold three ideas, or can only recall three easily, or some such stuff. I don't believe there is proof, whatever that would look like, that three ideas are best for a presentation. But I do know from practical experience that if you build your outline around more than four ideas, five tops, you have not worked hard enough to establish the core of your message.

Remember the description of presentations people hate and ones people don't. Somewhere in there is almost certainly going to be brevity as a quality that is attractive, and too much content as one that is not. Sticking to the discipline of having only four ideas in your outline will not make your presentation simplistic, it will make it simple, pared down, elegant. Try it – see what you find yourself.

THE INFORMATION TO COMMUNICATE IN YOUR PRESENTATION

You know a large amount about the subject of your presentation. That's why you are doing it. In the case of an IPO, you know about your company, the market, customers, etc. Your audience also know a significant amount about the subject of your presentation – which is why they are there. In terms of the IPO, the audience know about: companies in general, finance, financial markets, and so on. And some of that knowledge is shared, some is different.

The audience have an aim. To satisfy that, you have to communicate some knowledge to them. You too have an objective. In order to achieve it, there is another subset of your knowledge to communicate to them. So the information to communicate in your presentation is: (deep breath) the information you know, which your audience wants to know, in order for them to achieve their aim, which will also enable you to achieve your objective. Present that to them, and everyone will be happy.

So how do you establish what that information is?

DISCOVER THE OUTLINE OF YOUR PRESENTATION

My coachees and I have evolved a way to do this over the years. It is not necessarily right, but it works for me, and for some of them. That said, I think no two people end up doing it the same way. Each makes it their own, adapting what follows to their own way of working.

We use spider diagrams and other tools and techniques. You start by surfacing what you know about the subject using one spider diagram, then use a second to dig deeper into the subject so you reveal what it is really about. Bring Your Intention into the process in order to discover what to communicate to satisfy both the audience and yourself, and finally establish the best order to put this information in to communicate effectively with the audience. All this doesn't take long – half an hour at most.

SPIDER DIAGRAM 1

To do a spider diagram, you simply put the main subject in the centre, and write whatever comes into your mind around it. You connect what I'll call these topics – that is big ideas – to the main subject by lines. Smaller ideas go around topics, linked to them by lines.

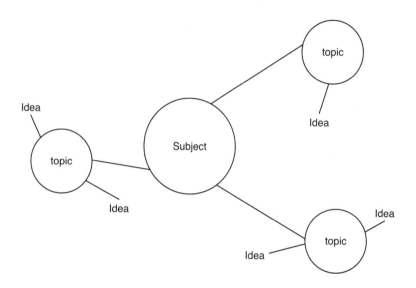

For this first spider diagram, write your Audience Objective in the middle of a large piece of paper – at least A4 – and, working swiftly, jot all your thoughts down around it.

BENEFIT OF USING A SPIDER DIAGRAM

One of the benefits of a spider diagram is that it is not linear, with one idea leading to, and suggesting, the next. At this stage of **O**utline, you want – in an easy way – to be able to look at all your ideas on the subject, to know what it is that you know about it.

Another advantage of a spider diagram is that it's quick, so you don't have to invest too much time in it. All you're doing is jotting key words on a sheet of paper. It also does not have to be neat and orderly – it's just a picture. Changing it isn't a big deal. You just add ideas as they occur to you, linking them to whichever topic you feel they link to. Finally, it is a superb way for a group to work together. You all just add ideas to the spider diagram as they occur to you until you judge it to be complete.

In a sense, a spider diagram, which is a simple visualization of your thoughts, enables you to have a dialogue with them.

Here's what Mike and David produced the first time we did this.

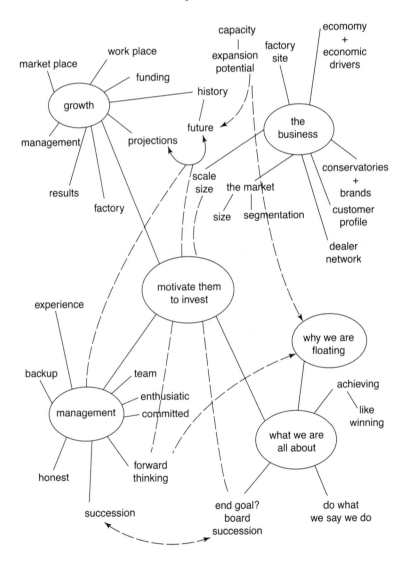

What do you notice about it?

What is most obvious is that it's a jumble. That's fine – this is a big subject, there's lots to say, both men are passionate about it, there's a considerable amount of money riding on the outcome. There are also dotted lines as well as unbroken ones. I ask people to put dotted lines in whenever an idea is linked to more than one topic.

Action Step: Do a spider diagram

Do a spider diagram now for your presentation. Do not strive to get it right – there is no 'right' here. Instead, note down everything as it occurs to you. Spend only a few minutes on it. Let the ideas flow out of you onto the paper, or trickle carefully if that's more your style. Whatever. But try to get it all down.

Read on only when you are done.

DUMP

I call this first spider diagram 'Dump', because that's what it is – a brain dump. Let's construct a presentation based on the Clearlight Dump spider diagram above.

Imagine you are a banker. Into the room walk Mike and David. You have 45 minutes with them and you are wondering, 'Do I invest in these guys?' If you invest and the company is a good one, its success will contribute to the progression of your career. If you invest and it bombs, it'll damage your fund, which will eventually damage your reputation. You're tired, stressed and you've got three more of these meetings before you get back to the office where you will have 32 voice mails, 154 unread emails . . . you get the picture.

Are you ready? Let's go.

> *'Good morning everyone. My name's Mike Smith, I'm CEO of Clearlight, and this is David Jones our Chief Finance Officer. We're going to tell you today about our company. We're going to start by outlining how we founded the company, how we grew it, and its current structure.*
>
> *We're then going to explain about ourselves, the directors, and then move on to our Senior Management Team. I think you'll be impressed at the quality of people we've assembled.*
>
> *Then I'm going to outline how we see the conservatory market, and our 30 years experience of it.'*

Let's pause here and check in on your inner reaction. Are you actively looking forward to the next 20 minutes? Personally, I'm beginning to get the familiar feelings of nausea as I contemplate the dreary trudge that is unfolding ahead of me. That's because this is the start of a school essay. It's got everything in it. It is worthy, and demonstrates to you that Mike and David know their stuff, and are diligent. If I was a banker, I might well just interrupt them and ask them questions rather than suffer through it.

It is, literally, a mind dump. It's as though those who base their presentations on this material are taking the contents of their minds, putting them in a bucket, and then pouring them in a steady stream over their audience's heads. Here, you sort it out.

THE REASON TO DO A DUMP SPIDER DIAGRAM

If it's so bad, why do I encourage people to do this initial spider diagram? It's because there's a quirk of human nature that makes this a useful tool. Imagine you have an important meeting to attend. On the way there, you get stuck for an hour in a tunnel. Even though you planned to be early, you are going to be at least half an hour late and because there's no mobile signal, you can't even explain to those you will be meeting what the problem is.

The logical thing to do when you finally arrive is to nod at everyone, mutter a quick apology, sit down and let things continue. That way you won't waste any more of everyone's time. But if you do that, you will probably find some of your mind distracted by the desire to explain what happened, to make it clear that you were unavoidably delayed, and that you did not call out of disrespect, but because calling was impossible. So what most of us do is explain what happened. Everyone round the table nods and makes sympathetic noises. If they have had any experience of life, they too have been in similar situations. Everyone relaxes, and the meeting can move forward with your full attention.

It's like that with a Dump spider diagram. Part of your mind is desperate to show all it knows about the subject of the presentation. Desperate to communicate. If you don't let it do so, it may well disturb you. The Dump spider diagram lets it communicate. The process of clearing your mind is a vital function of the Dump spider diagram. With the knowledge of your subject that is screaming to be communicated to the world out there, you will be able to think more clearly.

The Dump spider diagram has another use. That is represented by the ideas that are joined by dotted lines to several other ideas or topics. These are significant – and a potential problem. That's because a presentation – a good one, at any rate – is not a monologue, it is a virtual dialogue.

PRESENTATION AS VIRTUAL DIALOGUE

You, the presenter, speak. Your audience, your knowledgeable, insightful, adult audience, get what you're saying and immediately think of the implications. If the presentation is well constructed, a question will form in their minds about these. At which point, as if by magic, you will address that question. Your 'answer' to their inner question will prompt another query or insight in them, which you will deftly pick up with the next thing you say.

This is the basic dance of any good story, and the way narrative works. The storyteller says something and the listener thinks, 'What next?' And the next is supplied, prompting another 'What next?' The dialogue is virtual because, in many presentations, the party you are talking to, the audience, doesn't say anything until the end.

HOW LINKED IDEAS IMPAIR
THE VIRTUAL DIALOGUE

The virtual dialogue, however, stutters when one idea is linked to two possible others. Let's imagine a presentation done by Pete to a project group considering the outsourcing of some work. Pete is in management, and there are staff representatives in the audience. They know that the project means there will be job cuts, but they are going along for the moment because they know that if the cost base of the company does not reduce, there won't be any jobs at all in the near future.

One topic in Pete's presentation is how surprisingly cheap the bids are from a particular overseas manufacturer. This leads, in his Dump spider diagram, to two ideas: the company could increase profit, or it could reduce the size of the workforce here more than expected. This presents Pete with a dilemma. Which of the two ideas does he choose to mention directly after explaining the surprising cheapness of the quote? Whichever he chooses will leave the audience wondering about the other. Exaggerating slightly, the interplay between Pete's presentation and their thoughts might go along these lines.

Pete: I have to report that Sunshine Enterprises have quoted an astoundingly low price of only 10 cents a unit.

Audience (thinks): That's low!

Pete: That means we have the potential to make more margin – or could consider more job cuts here than we anticipated.

So far, so good. His presentation is keeping pace with their thoughts.

Pete: Turning first to the profit potential . . .

Audience: Those job losses sound bad.

And now they are thinking whatever they are thinking.

OR:

Pete: Turning first to the impact this might have on jobs.

Audience: Wow, that's potentially a lot of profit.

And, as before, their thoughts go wherever they go.

In that instant, while Pete's audience is wandering, they aren't attending to what he's actually saying. But, of course, he's still talking. So let's tune back in to Pete.

Pete: . . . 45% in the second year if we go with Option A.

What? We missed a bit of what Pete was saying, so what he's now saying is hard to understand. If he's lucky, and his audience is committed to understanding him, they'll persevere and pick up the thread again. If he or they are not, they won't. Their thoughts will continue to drift. They'll now miss a whole chunk of what he's saying, which will markedly reduce its impact.

That's the problem with linked ideas. They do, however – at this stage of GOER – have a powerful use.

HOW LINKED IDEAS ARE USEFUL

Linked ideas are useful because they show the underlying structure of the information you are communicating to the audience. I believe all information has some underlying structure. Normally we don't need to bother with it. We can all usefully work at the level of detail. But if we are to communicate effectively to others, it is useful to know the whole, and how our bit fits into it. Imagine the information you are trying to communicate is in the form of an elephant. Each of us is a proverbial blind people around it, encountering different parts. I feel its leg, you feel its tail, someone else feels its trunk, and so on. If I were to communicate to you simply from my understanding, I might describe this beast in terms of a tree trunk. You'd be confused – you experience it as some sort of rope. What's needed is for me to step back, and discover the whole, and how each part relates to that. Then I can communicate the sort of beast we are all dealing with. In terms of information, the dotted lines on the Dump spider diagram yield vital clues to this structure.

For example, in the Clearlight Dump spider diagram, the interconnected subjects are 'the future' and 'why we are floating'. Look at what points to 'the future': end goal, board succession, forward thinking, expansion capacity. And to 'why we are floating': forward thinking, what we are all about, expansion potential. When Mike and David focused on these two subjects, they realized that they were, in fact, central to their message. And, in some way, they are the same idea, one of *the* major ideas in their presentation – much more significant than the make-up of the Board, the workforce and all the other stuff that had previously been of such importance to them.

This, then, is the next step. Notice the interconnected ideas in your Dump spider diagram, put it aside and do a new one, also with the Audience Objective in the centre, but this time with the interconnected ideas as your topics. You are aiming this time to limit yourself to four or five topics at most.

If you've only got one or two interconnected ideas on your Dump spider diagram, you can decide the subject of the other topics when you are in the flow of doing this second spider diagram.

Action Step: Do a second spider diagram
Examine your own Dump spider diagram. Which ideas (if any) are most interconnected? Can you spot interconnections between ideas you previously overlooked? If so, put them in with dotted lines.

Now get another large sheet of paper, at least A4, and write the Audience Objective in the middle.

Holding these interlinked topics in your mind, take a breath and go for it. Let the ideas flow out of you onto the paper. Don't think too much, just enjoy.

Here's the second spider diagram that Mike and David produced.

It has just four main topics. Reading clockwise from top left they are: the future; the past up to date; the business; reasons for the float. Mike realized that this is quite a good story structure: the past . . . i.e. how we started; the present . . . i.e.

the business as it is now, plus reasons for the float; and the future. They were thrilled. They immediately felt that this was a huge improvement on their original presentation.

What about you? Put yourself in a banker's shoes. What do you feel when you run this presentation through your mind. It begins with guys who are passionate about their business giving you a potted history of how they grew it; focuses then on what a success it is at the moment and the enormous opportunities they see as possible if they had the funds to grab them; and the fat returns you are going to make. How was that? Got your interest? If it has, that's excellent.

Er, no. Because, while this second spider diagram – which I call 'Dig' as it represents you digging deeper into your mind than with Dump – might deliver on the audience's objective, it doesn't necessarily deliver on yours. That's because you haven't included your own intention in your thinking. To do that, you have to be able to communicate two ideas simultaneously.

COMMUNICATING TWO IDEAS SIMULTANEOUSLY

You want to be able to say one thing, and have the audience understand it, plus this other meaning, Your Intention. It's like conveying two pictures at once using only one image. One way of doing that would be to have a main picture – a landscape, or something – and cut around it so that it was in the shape of the second picture – a human profile perhaps. Now you are visually communicating two pictures simultaneously. In a sense, that's what a good presenter does in a presentation. They communicate information – the various ideas in the spider diagrams so far – but only that information which builds up, in the audience's mind, the picture of the human profile. At some point the audience will recognize the silhouette and realize 'Ah ha! That's the real meaning of this presentation.' They'll be satisfied because they've understood what you are saying at meaning level, and – here's the real bonus – that meaning will be much stronger in their mind than all the detailed stuff you've been telling them. And you'll have controlled the meaning they take from your presentation, so it is not random, as it is with all too many poor presentations. We are, in fact, expert at doing this.

Imagine Dolores DID want to go out with Brad. Further, let's imagine she was, truly and unavoidably, busy this week and the next. How might their dialogue go now?

He asks her out for this weekend. What might she say? How about, 'Unfortunately I'm busy this weekend'? What about next weekend? 'I'm busy next weekend too.' Same information – I can't go out with you for the next couple of weekends – but if Brad is listening with any care, he'll have understood something different. What is that? Isn't it, ask me out for a date the weekend **after** next and I'll say yes. He might even try for a date mid-week.

How did Dolores convey that meaning to Brad? She used some key words and phrases. 'Unfortunately' is a major clue. And the phrase 'this weekend' and 'next weekend' was a clear signal to him to ask for the weekend after that. And the fact that, given her busy life, she was willing to sacrifice her weekends so far ahead was also significant. She likes you, Brad. Go for it lad.

In terms of presentations and GOER, I call those words and phrases 'magic words'. They are what enable us to communicate our meaning. I have developed a tool to discover those magic words. To understand how it works, we need to consider the phenomena of conditioning minds.

CONDITIONING YOUR MIND

Robert Cialdini, in his superb book *Influence, Science and Practice* (published by Allyn and Bacon, with my edition being from 2001) describes something discovered by the owner of a shop selling pool tables. In the USA, people sometimes buy pool tables for use in the home. To maximize sales, which would you put nearest the door: the cheapest, or the most expensive? Most people believe it should be the cheapest, to entice the customer in. That was standard practice in the pool table retail trade until this particular pool shop owner decided to experiment. He put the most expensive ones by the door. What do you imagine happened? In fact, the shop sold more tables, at a higher average cost.

What's happening here? It's that the minds of the customers were being conditioned. With the cheap pool tables by the door, people walk in and think 'a couple of hundred dollars (or whatever) for a pool table. That's not too bad.' They walk on and encounter the more expensive tables. 'A thousand dollars a table. That's a lot to spend on what is just a hobby.' The high end tables in the back of the store, for many tens of thousands of dollars, are clearly totally irrelevant. So they return to the front of the store and buy one of the low end tables.

With the tables the other way round, something very different happens. The customer enters and encounters tables costing tens of thousands of dollars. That's obviously way out of their league, but – hey – they're lovely tables. Next they encounter tables for a thousand dollars. Still good tables, but not quite so wonderful. Further into the store, there are tables for a couple of hundred dollars. They're clearly rubbish, so people return to the mid-range ones and buy one of those.

Stretch

Pay attention, when you are shopping, to how this phenomenon works. Notice how fancy clothes shops put their best, most expensive clothes in the window. Notice what it does to your frame of mind as you enter the shop and look at the clothes there.

So how does this work with presentations?

TWO IDEAS IN A PRESENTATION

Charles had a presentation to do that had an interesting underlying meaning. He was in an unpleasant situation. The previous MD of his company, the UK subsidiary of a major multinational, had split the operation into two: an Importer and a Retailer. The Importer traded with the parent; the Retailer bought product off the Importer and sold it to outlets which dealt with the public.

This may have made sense on paper, but in reality it was a disaster. The easiest way for the Importer to hit its ambitious profit targets was by refusing to negotiate with the Retailer. The Retailer, in a fiercely competitive market, could not raise prices to the outlets. Result: the Retailer was squeezed of profits and was failing. Charles was the Retailer's Chief Financial Officer, the CFO.

A SWAT team of senior executives had been sent by the parent company to the UK to discover what was going on. Charles was tasked with presenting this year's horrible figures to them. Instead of the projected profit of several millions, they were going to be lucky to break even. The Audience Objective for his presentation? To find out what was going on with the UK retailer. Charles's Intention? He'd had some problems with this. He knew he did not want to go with his boss's idea, which was to promise that next year things would be better. They wouldn't be. He did not want to go with the Group CFO's idea, to blame the bad conditions in the UK market. That would also send, Charles felt, the wrong message. He went round the Five Whys several times and, eventually, the process threw up an answer. His intention was to explain that unless the situation was fixed, the Retailer would go bankrupt.

Referring back to the three-level listening (see page 14 of Chapter 2) that can be represented as:

Hear =	Audience Objective =	Results for this year = Figures, charts, trends
↓	↓	↓
Listen =	**Magic Words**	?
↓	↓	↓
Meaning =	Your Intention	Fix the underlying problem or we go bankrupt

At the hearing level, the audience want their objective satisfied. They want to hear the results for this year, to have the figures explained to them. At the meaning level, Charles wants to communicate his intention: fix the situation or bad things will happen. The blanks at the listening level will be filled in with the magic words. You establish them by using my tool, the Meaning Generator.

THE MEANING GENERATOR

You begin by writing Your Intention in the middle of a blank sheet of paper. In Charles's case this was:

Unless you fix the situation, we will go bankrupt

Now, divide Your Intention into functional groups of words – words that go together to make a thought:

Unless you fix the situation, we will go bankrupt

In other words, you don't divide 'go bankrupt' into 'go' and 'bankrupt' – they are one thought conveyed in two words.

Action Step: Use the Meaning Generator
Write Your Intention on a sheet of paper and divide it into functional units of words as above.

Above each functional unit of words on your sheet now write the words that spring into your mind when you look at them. In Charles's case, the word 'unless' made him think of 'until', which made him think of 'Sword of Damocles', and then 'never' and 'no choice'. The Sword of Damocles showed that in Charles's mind, this whole situation was just a disaster waiting to happen – that he/they had no real choice.

Continuing with Charles's Intention, when he thought of the word 'you' in this situation he came up with:

the parent company
the board
those responsible
the cause
us

He got to that final word – 'us' – by thinking of the opposite of 'you'. Thinking of opposites often helps generate ideas when using this tool. So if stuck for words to come up with around 'sell', you might think of its opposite, which for you might be 'buy': the opposite of which might be 'give away'; the opposite of which might be for you 'barter', etc. Each of these words might be a magic word for your presentation.

When Charles had finished with the 'Meaning Generator' his page looked like this.

		Structural	
		Not sticking plaster	
Never	Us	Sort it out	
Until	The cause	Mend	The arrangement
Sword of	Those responsible	Repair	The relationship
Damocles	The parent	Tinker	The mess
No choice	company	Change	The split
Unless	**you**	**fix**	**the situation**
we		**will**	**go bankrupt**
The retailer	Inevitable		Fail
The company	The future		Redundancies
The importer	No escape		Legal liability
Us	Procrastinate		Collapse
			Fallout
			Haemorrhage

Action Step: Complete your own Meaning Generator
Write Your Intention on the middle of a sheet of A4. Divide the phrase into functional groups. Look at each word or group of words for a few seconds. What similar words jump into your mind? Write them on the paper. What are the opposites? Write them all down too. And – if you want – the opposites of the opposites. Move to the

next group till you have processed it all. Don't worry if you blank on a word or functional group, leave it and move on. Go back to it later as you practice and gain confidence with this exercise.

THE MAGIC WORDS

To see what you've got through doing this exercise, try this experiment. Imagine you were a member of the parent company of Charles's UK subsidiary. You've come to the country to kick ass, to find out what those wasters in Retail are doing. You're expecting them to grovel, to make excuses, to promise to work harder next year, to lash the troops and get performance out of them. You go to a presentation, and imagine you heard some of these words from Charles:

> *'The cause is the relationship, the split. Tinkering, sticking plasters, from the parent company, inevitable haemorrhage, redundancies, collapse, bankruptcy legal liability.'*

What are you hearing? Is it something like this: 'You, the parent company, have got to fix this situation, not just tinker with it'? 'If you don't, the loss of money will continue and we'll go bankrupt and you'll be liable.'

Action Step: Do a third spider diagram
Read the magic words you've written around Your Intention to yourself until you feel your mind is filled with them. Now take a new sheet of paper and write the Audience Objective in the middle. Read it once and swiftly do a third spider diagram. Write the four – or at most five – topics onto your spider diagram. Then list any ideas which relate to the topics.

CLARIFY SPIDER DIAGRAM

This is the final spider diagram, which I call 'Clarify'. It is usually simple, clear and robust (see the Clearlight spider diagram illustration below). It consists just of those subjects that you want to communicate to the audience to satisfy their objective and AT THE SAME TIME deliver on Your Intention. It usually has no linked ideas, and no lists of ideas.

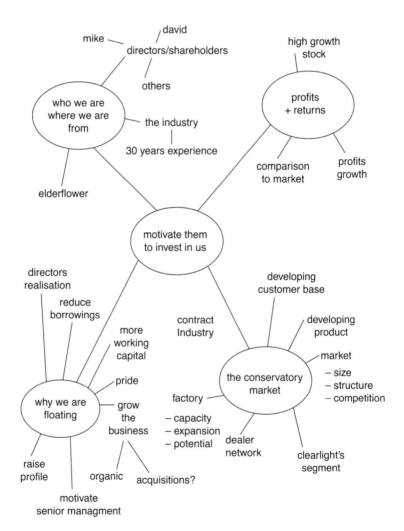

TIME TAKEN TILL NOW ON OUTLINE

It might seem as if **O**utline takes a long time because it involves several activities which take some explanation. But how long do you think it will take to do once you know this technique?

Dump spider diagram: 10 minutes, tops. Once you become adept at spider diagrams, half that.
Dig spider diagram: let's err on the side of generosity, 10 minutes.
Meaning Generator: 5 minutes?
Clarify spider diagram: 5 minutes.

Total: maximum half an hour. With a bit of practice, 15 minutes, tops.

Result? You now know the core of your presentation, the four or at most five topics which, when presented to your audience, will deliver on their objective and on yours.

Now to sort out the best order in which to put these topics.

LINEAR ORDER

A presentation exists in time. One unit of information is followed by another until the whole is finished. This has profound implications.

Suppose you want to communicate something to the audience that is, in terms of information, shaped like a dumbbell. In other words, there are two spherical blocks of dense information, connected by a long, slim rod of sequential information. Because a presentation is spoken – it exists in time – you can't just transfer the whole lot to your audience at once. You have to break the dumbbell of information up into pieces (which is what you're doing when you do the spider diagrams); and pass it to the audience, piece by piece, with instructions on how to reassemble it themselves.

Let's look at that process from the audience's point of view. They receive various pieces of information from you. They examine each in turn, accept, question or reject it, and then attempt to fit them back together to make a coherent shape. If you communicate clearly, a lot of them will manage to reassemble, in their heads, something that looks vaguely like the dumbbell you started with. They'll have understood not just the detail of what you're saying, but the bigger picture.

A good presenter can pass the audience the pieces in the right order. In the case of information in the shape of a dumbbell, it might be sensible to first pass the audience the pieces that make up one weight; then pass them the pieces that make up the bar; only then to pass them the pieces of the other weight which goes on the other end of the rod. An incompetent way to do it would be to pass the audience all the pieces that make up both weights in one go, and only then pass them the pieces that make up the dumbbell bar. Worse would be to jumble the dumbbell pieces and the rod pieces together. The audience would have a much harder struggle with such communications, even though the pieces were the same.

Another factor that influences linear order is that each unit of information causes the audience to ponder in different ways. Getting the order right is critical if the virtual dialogue is to flow smoothly, and not grind to a halt at any stage.

LINEAR ORDER AND
THE VIRTUAL DIALOGUE

A practical example might make this clearer. Imagine your-self as a worker employed by the only large business in a small town which is miles from anywhere. You are one of the few lucky ones: you've got a well-paid, secure job.

Your boss calls the whole workforce together. What follows are two ways the presentation might go. I include only the start, because that determines what comes next. Decide which works better for you.

> ### Linear Order 1
> *'I've asked you to gather here today because I'm afraid I've got some bad news. We're going to have to make half of you redundant.'*

Are you going to listen to whatever the boss says next, or are you going to be thinking: please, let it not be me, let me be in the half that is still employed here?

Now for the alternative order.

> ### Linear Order 2
> *'I've asked you to gather here today to tell you about the situation the company is in. It is important that you understand it, to understand the actions we're going to have to take.'*

Are you going to listen to whatever the boss says next? Personally, I suspect that with a start like this, I'd be all ears, aware that something important is going to be communi-cated. In other words, Linear Order 1 will fail no matter what information is in it. The same information, presented in a different order – as in Linear Order 2 – will succeed. And here's the trick. You want to arrange the information in the right order not for you, but for your audience. And that's the next crucial topic to understand.

THE CURSE OF KNOWLEDGE

Chip and Dan Heath, in their lovely book *Made to Stick* (about how to communicate memorable messages) identify a problem they call the 'Curse of Knowledge'. When you know something, it can be hard to remember what it feels like to be someone who doesn't know it. Remember also that your audience aren't idiots. They know lots about the subject – but different lots from you. That creates a problem.

Imagine you are driving to a meeting in the country. You stop a local to ask directions. If the local is not a skilled communicator, they might say something like this.

> *'Go down the hill till you get to Flatterys, head up the old road to the school house, then go down towards the Fire Station.'*

WHAT? Flatterys? The old road? Is there a new one that I shouldn't take? How do I recognize 'the school house'? And where's the Fire Station? A local – indeed, this local – would understand exactly what he said, precisely because a local knows the area. But someone who was not local is, literally, lost.

So how do you, cursed with your knowledge of your subject, discover the linear order that works best for your audience? Easy. You just ask them.

RESEARCHING THE LINEAR ORDER WITH YOUR AUDIENCE

To do this effectively, it's best to construct two linear orders and ask your audience which works best for them. Why two? Why not just present them with one and ask them what they'd think?

What do you think they would say if you just called them with one linear order and asked them their opinion? Wouldn't they just say 'That's great!' The reason for that?

a) To get on with their work as quickly as possible, and
b) So as not to risk saying something that might upset you.

It's so much easier just to compliment someone than to get into what could be an unpleasant conversation.

Offering two choices changes the situation:

a) They can't so easily terminate the conversation. If they say they like them both, you could ask them what they like better about each, and what they disliked. Also,
b) By offering two alternatives, you are implicitly saying that you are not married to either. That gives them permission to comment in any way on them – confident that you are not going to burst into tears.

The key to making this conversation successful is not to give the person you are talking to a clue as to which order you prefer.

So, here's how Mike of Clearlight did it. His Clarify spider diagram had four topics on it:

1.   Who we are.
2.   Profits and returns.
3.   The conservatory market.
4.   Why we are floating.

The above is the linear order that seemed most logical to him. Just out of interest, it was also the way the Clarify spider diagram was created, logically, starting top left-hand corner and proceeding round clockwise.

The second linear order has to be properly jumbled up, not just slightly shuffled. This is what we came up with:

1.   The conservatory market.
2.   Why we are floating.
3.   Who we are.
4.   Profits and returns.

Initially, that second, jumbled linear order made no sense at all to Mike or David. But it is your job to make sense of it in order to do your audience research authentically. You have to appear to believe that both are equally strong. If the person you are talking to picks up a clue from you about which you prefer, they may be tempted to take the easy option and feedback to you what they think you want them to say.

So, before having this conversation, Mike put a moment's work into constructing a story around that second linear order. It wasn't so difficult. It begins with how Clearlight sees the conservatory market: how it is divided, the main product groups, who supplies what. This leads naturally into the opportunities Clearlight see out there – opportunities which require capital, which is (of course) why we are floating. Next topic is – naturally – who we are because anyone thinking of investing in us would need to know that. Finally, in order to invest, you'd want to know the profits and returns we're making currently. Put like that, this second linear order doesn't sound so bad, does it? In particular, the idea of leaving them thinking about money seems a smart move.

So, when I left Mike and David, they promised to make a few calls and discover the optimal linear order. When I returned, Mike reported that the calls had been, well, shocking. They hadn't gone to plan at all. It seems he'd got halfway through the first when his accountant (who had been an investment banker in his youth) interrupted him. 'You're starting in the wrong place. The first thing they'll want to know about is you and Elderflower.' Elderflower? What was that? Mike and David looked very uncomfortable, then Mike 'fessed up. It seems that Mike and David had met when young men, employed by a conservatory company called Elderflower. Elderflower had been founded, and was led, by an older, charismatic man. He had successfully floated the venture – and run off with the funds. In its day, it had been a considerable scandal. They hadn't mentioned it to me, or planned to bring it up in front of their audience, because – as Mike explained – they didn't want to bring up an irrelevant subject that might spook potential investors.

The trouble is, as Mike's accountant had pointed out, it was anything but irrelevant to investors. Anyone remotely interested in the opportunity would do their research and pretty much the first thing they'd find would be Mike and David's link to Elderflower. If it wasn't mentioned up front in the presentation, it would destroy their credibility. Together, in 5 minutes, Mike and his accountant had worked out a third linear order:

1. Who we are (including their non-involvement with the Elderflower fraud).
2. The market and how Clearlight fits into it.
3. Profits and returns to date.
4. Why we are floating.

A convert to research, Mike had tried out his three linear orders on a couple of other potential members of the audience and all had found the third the most effective.

This salutary tale illustrates a vital point. You are doing this research not to get applause for your creativity, but to get input from your audience. Should you be fortunate enough to have them tell you a better way to organize your material, LISTEN TO THEM!! Thank them. They are doing you a huge favour. In a conversation lasting a few minutes, they are enabling you to hurdle the Curse of Knowledge.

Note that this third linear order has the clarity of the first, and brings the conversation about money closer to the end as in the second. Once he recognized this, Mike realized that he could do the first two topics – they were his natural territory – and David would be better placed to do the last two, since they were both about money. Suddenly the fact that two of them were going to be in the presentation made 'dramatic' sense. They were a double act. We also realized that their sharing the burden of doing the presentation was the best way they could communicate 'us' to the audience (as in 'to motivate them to invest in *us*').

Note too that we – Mike, David and I – did not come up with this order and, even if we had, we'd have been hard pushed to choose between it and the other linear orders. If we hadn't gone back to the audience and asked for their input, we'd have had to resort to one of those endless debates where we attempted to justify and measure the merits of each of our personal favourites. You won't always have such a dramatic intervention from the audience. Here's a little technique I use when the response is more muted.

MARKS OUT OF TEN

I occasionally find it useful when I am researching a presentation to ask someone to give what I'm proposing a mark out of ten. Ironic, really, that this school-based way of giving feedback is useful – but it is. We have a shared understanding of it. When someone gives you a mark – say, seven out of ten – you've got several options. One is to ask if that is sufficient. After all, they might be a hard marker. Another is to ask what might raise the mark. They'll usually supply marvellous ideas.

Finally, if you feel seven is not OK, and do more work on the idea, pitch it again to the same person. You've now got a definite scale with which to evaluate this new version. If they give anything above seven, you're moving in the right direction.

Action Step: Construct two linear orders
Construct two alternative linear orders for your own presentation by writing the topics in your Clarify spider diagram in two orders – one you like that makes obvious 'logical' sense to you, and one that seems weird. Then work out how you are going to pitch both to a couple of members of your audience as if you liked each equally, and make the phone calls. It often helps to pitch the alternative order first.

Do your best to make the conversation light, so they're encouraged to engage with you. Listen carefully to what they say, action it and decide on an optimal linear order.

THE MATERIAL YOU LEAVE OUT

At this point in my workshops, I often notice a pained look on one or more of the participant's faces. When I ask about it, I get something like this. *'Yes, this "optimal linear order" works – up to a point. But what about all this other great stuff I know? If I were to include it, the presentation would surely work even better, be even more convincing.'*

Er, no. 'This other great stuff I know' is knowledge only you, the person speaking, cares about. It is likely to be at best irrelevant, and at worst tedious, to communicate it to the audience. How do I know? When you did your research on the linear orders, the audience didn't say, 'You've left out a crucial bit of information', or puzzle over a jump in the narrative. If they had noticed a lack, they'd have mentioned it – as they did in the Clearlight example.

Remember, the key characteristic of a fine presentation is Enough, not More. If, on the day, someone in the audience wants to know about 'the other great stuff' you know, they'll ask you about it. That is, after all, why you've left a chunk of time for Q&As. And, when they do, and you supply an interesting and informative answer, they'll realize that you are wearing your knowledge lightly – that, although you know a ton of stuff, you put work into presenting them with what they needed to know, and no more. This realization too will enhance, rather than diminish, their opinion of you.

Stretch

Experiment with taking more and more out of your emails. You may well discover, as many people do, that up to a certain point, the more you take out, the more powerful a sentence or a thought becomes when communicated to others.

And, if you are wondering, this exercise enabled Charles to deliver a rather surprising presentation to the SWAT team. He told me that, on the day, he found himself filled with energy and a sense of purpose as he got ready to do the presentation. A pivotal moment came when – as he took them through a particularly gruesome set of figures – one of the visitors groaned. Charles spontaneously said, 'If you think that's bad, wait till you see the next slide.' What a fabulous message that aside delivered. It said Charles had nothing to lose, was not apologizing and was going to give it to his audience straight.

At the end, instead of administering a kicking, the Board's SWAT team rolled up their sleeves and started a serious conversation with the Retailer about how the underlying situation could be rectified. Charles's boss congratulated him later for doing what he felt was the best presentation he'd ever experienced in his long business career. Charles was a star.

BALANCE BETWEEN AUDIENCE OBJECTIVE AND YOUR INTENTION

There is no 'rule' about how clearly or subtly to communicate Your Intention. It is pragmatic: what matters is that it gets across. Some people need messages to be spelt out, some don't. Culture plays a part here too. Some prefer explicit messages, for others, a hint is enough. Again, your research – your actual, detailed knowledge of your audience – is your infallible guide.

GOER AND CUSTOMER CARE

GOER, as a process, embodies the message that, for you, customer needs are paramount. If the person or people you have done your research with are in the audience when you do your presentation, they'll notice that you listened to them. No need now to labour the point that you 'listen to customers'. No need either to spend much time explaining that 'customer care is a core value' – you have demonstrated that too.

SUMMARY

How long will this take? Half an hour, max, to get to your Clarify spider diagram. Then two linear orders and a couple of phone calls. All done in under an hour. In a short time you have established the four, at most five, topics which, when presented to your audience in the right order, will deliver on their objective, and on your intention. You are now ready to 'write' your presentation. Except that many people familiar with GOER do not write at all. More of that in the next chapter, Elaborate.

Elaborate

4

This is the creative stage of GOER. When I say this in workshops, I see the blood drain from some people's faces. The very idea of creativity terrifies many of us. Here's the good news. 'Creativity' – at least in terms of presentations – is a learnable skill like any other: cooking, playing tennis, doing Sudoku. The more you practice, and the more you apply good techniques to it, i.e. ones that are set out in this chapter, the better you'll get at it.

Secondly, you don't have to be especially 'creative' for your presentation to work. After all, people are coming to your presentation partly to meet you. They don't require a hugely creative act. All you have to do at **E**laborate is flesh out the ideas in your optimal linear order in a way that is true to yourself.

Thirdly, you are using GOER – not the School Essay Technique – so you don't need to write anything at this stage. All that is required is that you imagine your presentation in detail and make notes to remind yourself of how you've elaborated it (which is part of the reason I call this stage 'elaborate' – as in 'ee-lab-or-ate' – rather than 'write'. The other part of the reason is that GOWR is a hopeless acronym.) Many people who use GOER *never* write their presentations. More on this later.

Before we plunge into the adventure that is **E**laborate, there are a couple of ideas to take on board.

THE IMPORTANCE OF YOUR FIRST TIME

The first time you elaborate your presentation is precious. You want to make this 'first draft' – which is what it would be if you were writing – as good as possible. Here's why.

Let's construct a sentence, at random, word by word. The only rule is that it must make sense.

First word:

> 'What' . . . ?

Next:

> 'What did' . . . ?

Next:

> 'What did the' . . . ?

> 'What did the elephant' . . . ?

OK. Did we have a large number of words to choose from for the first word of the sentence? Yes. Huge. Did we have an equally large number of words to choose from for the second word? No – only certain words fit after that first word. How many did we have to choose from for the third word compared with the second one? Fewer still. Do you recognize the shape of the numbers? It's a funnel, with fewer and fewer words to choose from as the sentence progresses. And as one sentence follows another, your choices narrow continuously. Not only is this a funnel, it's also worth noting that the words you choose at the start of the sentence exert an influence on all the ones that follow. And the first sentence exerts an influence on the second, and the first paragraph on all subsequent ones, and so on.

It's like a walk into a forest of information. Your first steps begin to define the path you are taking. Every step after that influences every next step. The path you tread defines both where you go, and where you don't go. Which is why word processing is so dangerous. Many people seem to believe that you can just bung any old words into the computer and then, using the power that word processing offers, edit your text till it works. Sadly, even when you edit, the ghostly presence of the words that preceded the words that you are editing remains. That's why, if you attempt to construct a coherent piece by editing together lumps from different documents, it works so badly. Each lump has been formed by the text preceding it. Hack it out and attempt to bolt it together out of context and – no matter what you do – the joins will show. Even if only on a subconscious level. The piece will always remain clunky.

Moral: if you want to create a good communication, in any medium, you have to make as good a first shot at it as you can.

How we talk
When we talk, we're doing something extraordinarily complex, even if – mostly – we take it completely for granted. It's similar to the process of writing (Chapter 1). Put simply, it's something like this. We have a thought. For most of us, that's a vague feeling somewhere inside us. By focusing on that vague feeling, we can form it into words – or, at least, into a few words that start what we're going to say. We know what we mean, but the end of the sentence is too far away to plan. Then we fill our lungs with air and carefully expel it past our vocal chords, which have to be shaped to turn that air into sounds. As the sounds emerge into our mouths, our tongues, teeth, lips and cheeks work to convert those sounds into words.

While we're doing all that, our minds are racing ahead, sorting out the grammar of our sentence so that we continue to express the original thought we had. And we have to do all this while monitoring the reaction of those we are communicating with, and attempting to scan ahead in our minds for the next thing we are going to say, all without falling over. Is it any wonder that we so often say things that surprise even ourselves? It's a living process, one that exists in time, in flow.

What we don't do, at least what most of us don't typically do, is think a whole sentence then say it. That's why creativity is a performance. As you start to elaborate the ideas in Outline, one word will spark off another. Sentences will flow. Words will clothe the scaffolding that is your optimal linear order (and that last sentence was entirely a surprise to me when I wrote it, but I like it, so it's staying in). That's why I call this stage Elaborate – not write.

ELABORATE RATHER THAN WRITE

The alternative to writing is to imagine your presentation, in detail. This involves finding a way to flesh out your optimal linear order: to identify the examples you'll use, the facts and figures, the case studies, the jokes, the images. Once you've done this, the task then is to record that in some way. The aim at the end of this stage is to have a fairly clear and detailed idea of what you are going to say or do from the beginning of your presentation, through the middle, to the end.

You start by looking at your optimal linear order. Then imagine it, from the start to the end. Talk to yourself, hear what you're going to say, imagine the visuals (if any), consider the audience interactions. Allow yourself to enjoy the experience, to be surprised by what pops into your mind, welcome any insights, ideas, inspiration, phrases, examples. Record it if possible as you go along, or as soon after the session as possible so you don't lose any of this material. You can do this in notes, pictures, spider diagrams, handwritten scrawl, PowerPoint slides – even typing it into a word processor. Whatever you like, as long as the process of recording does not impede the flow.

Once you've done this, you have completed **E**laborate and are ready to move on to the next stage of GOER, **R**efine. Before you do this, a few notes.

DON'T GET IT RIGHT, GET IT WRITTEN

What this old scriptwriter's saying means is that, at a certain point – in the case of GOER, it's at **E**laborate – you have to actually get something done. Do it, and don't worry about whether or not it is 'right', by which is meant perfect, polished, with every last word correct. The stage of making what you have created right is **R**efine, the next stage. What you are looking for at **E**laborate is to get something 'written' – by which is meant, something decided about how the piece will flow, move, where it will go.

EXILE THE CRITIC

Another way of thinking about 'don't get it right' is to imagine the critic in your head – you know, the voice that tells you that what you are doing is no good – and thank it for helping to make your final product excellent, but invite it (temporarily) to leave the room, to stop watching what you are doing. The critic is not useful at **E**laborate. Reassure your critic: there'll be plenty for them to do at **R**efine.

SCHEDULING YOUR ELABORATE

Our energy varies through the day. 'Morning people' are highly energized at first, then gradually fade through the day. They have a peak some other time but – broadly – it's downhill after a bright start. Evening people gradually warm up through the day and end up energized. You can try to ignore this variation in your natural rhythm, or mask it with performance-enhancing drugs such as tea, coffee, chocolate and sugar, but it's there. Let's call the time when you are naturally most energized 'A' time and the time when your energy is naturally lowest 'C' time. Everything between is 'B' time. (I first encountered this idea in James Noon's book *'A' Time*, published by Chapman and Hall, my edition being 1991.)

I've asked people in workshops to estimate how much better they perform in their A time than normal, and the average seems to be 100% better. Similarly, they feel they perform 100% worse in their C time than normal. To be conservative, let's halve that: let's say that you are merely 100% better in A time than in C time. Here's the way that many people who don't know GOER write the first draft of their presentation. They're at their desks during their C time feeling dull and lifeless. They have deliberately left this time free because they know that if they go to a meeting now, they might doze off. They look at the tough jobs they have got to do, and can't be bothered. Their email inbox frightens them. What to do? 'I know!' they think. 'I'll just have a go at writing my presentation. It won't really matter what I write, I can just word process it later to make sense of it.'

Nooooo. Assuming the 100% difference between A and C time, whatever they elaborate in C time will be half as good as if they had done it in A time. And your first draft will set the tone for your presentation. If it is to be any good, you cannot afford to do this. So, what is a better way?

IDENTIFY YOUR A TIME

Many of us instinctively know when our A time is. If you don't, did you have a time in college when you chose to do your most difficult assignments? If so, that's likely to be your A time. If you are unlucky, it was late at night, so you'll probably want to find another burst of A time in the day. (My observation of myself suggests that we don't just have one A time in a day, but that our energy fluctuates several times throughout the hours we work, giving us several smallish periods of A time. In my case, they last no longer than one hour, and I have three of them, with the most intense, unfortunately, between 6.30 and 7.30 in the morning.)

One way to recognize A time is that this is when you find it's easiest to get into 'flow'. So being alert to flow is a good way to identify A time.

FLOW

This is when your attention focuses most easily on what you are doing and you find yourself working in a fluid and natural way, flowing – hence the term – through tasks. Many of us have experienced this, and it's a pleasant state to be in. Ideally, you will do the whole of Elaborate in your A time while you are in flow. You will simply start at the beginning of the optimal linear order and speed through to the end, easily and naturally.

Action Step: Identify your A time
One way to do this is to notice, over a couple of days, when you go into flow. A pattern should quickly emerge. Be quite specific. Not just 'morning', but the time in the morning, when it starts and when it ends.

Stretch
Decide that for a few days you are going to try to do important things in A time, and things where mistakes don't matter in C time (filing emails? Clearing your inbox? Networking?) Schedule everything else into B time. Experiment and see how this way of managing yourself in time changes the way your day feels, and your productivity.

PLACE

Many people find that they are most creative in a particular place. Roald Dahl famously wrote in a shed in his garden. Experiment with where you can be most creative in your A time. It might be a coffee bar, or your car, or the bath – wherever it is, go there to elaborate your presentation if possible.

Action Step: Identify where you like to be creative
Find where you most easily get into flow in order to elaborate your presentation. It can either be a place – Ric's Wine Bar, for instance – or a kind of place – perhaps any busy coffee bar where there's lots of different people around.

EXERCISE

Many people find that repetitive exercise helps the mind to freewheel and flow (think of poets wandering lonely as a cloud in order to compose verse). The sort of exercise that seems to help is dull and doesn't require that you pay much attention. Examples include jogging, swimming laps, circuits in the gym.

Action Step: Do some exercise in order to elaborate
Experiment with imagining a presentation while doing something repetitive and relatively mindless. You might surprise yourself.

PREPARE TONIGHT FOR TOMORROW

I find it an advantage to book my A time at least one day in advance if it is possible. In other words, I might decide on Wednesday evening that on Friday I'll elaborate a particular presentation, at my peak A time of 6.30 a.m., at my desk. By Thursday I'll often notice my mind is straying into the task. I'm starting to form phrases, get ideas. I just let it do that in the background, welcoming the fact that I'm already starting to process the task in what would otherwise just be down time. Often, I find myself waking with the job almost done. Yes! This is an entirely legitimate and healthy way to get more work out of yourself, without more effort. It's like using your computer to process a massive computation in those periods when you are not using it.

PROCRASTINATION

Occasionally I get to a block of A time and find the ideas are just not coming. Don't worry about this. You are not quite ready to do the job. If you want to accelerate the creative process, try more repetitive exercise to create the mental conditions for your mind to do its stuff. Walking helps me in this situation. If nothing comes yet, respect your system. It is on the job, marinating the task more thoroughly. When it comes up with the answer, it'll be good. But beware of distractions. Some people find, when they come to their A time, that there is an almost overwhelming urge to read their emails, or check their voice mail. RESIST. This is a dangerous distraction. Remind yourself that you have worked to free a block of A time, and trust that if you give it 5 minutes, something excellent will appear.

THIS IS NOT AN EXAM

You don't need to hurry once you are in A time and elaborating. Treat it as if you have all the time in the world. Relax. You may well amaze yourself by what you come up with. Many of my clients report that they have delighted themselves by their own ideas.

WHEN THERE'S NO A TIME

Occasionally we all have to do things in a hurry, and there may be no A time between now and when you need to elaborate. There's a whole chapter on how to deal with this (Chapter 7: In an Emergency).

WHEN A JOB IS TOO BIG TO COMPLETE IN A TIME

Occasionally you will be faced with the need to elaborate something that takes longer than one burst of A time. What I do in this situation is elaborate until I notice myself ceasing to be in flow. The symptoms of it are, in my case: I suddenly decide to check my emails, I get hungry, I need a hot drink, I start correcting myself and chopping and changing ideas. As soon as this happens, I stop. When my next A time is due, I clear my thoughts, stop answering the phone, close the email package and settle down to elaborate. Amazingly, my mind seems able to slot straight back into the job, picking up where I left off and allowing me to continue from where I stopped.

SIMPLE IS NOT EASY

Another thought on the word 'simple'. Simple is not easy. Think of the iPod, a beacon of simplicity in a sea of gadgets festooned with buttons and dials and sliders. If you can find a simple way to express yourself, that is to be celebrated.

The opposite of simple is complicated. If you find yourself getting complicated, step back and reconsider. Trust yourself: there is a simple way to express what you mean, and you will find it.

Stretch
Keep a pad, pen or pencil within arm's reach at all times (yes, even by your bed). Ideas can come to you at any time about a presentation you are working on, and – although when they occur to you, you may be convinced you can retain them – in the hurly burly of life it is all too easy to lose them. Capture them when they come to you. These messages are from your deeper self and are almost always worth passing on to your audience.

CREATIVE UNEASE

If you start to feel uncomfortable at the **E**laborate stage, that is entirely appropriate. Speaking for myself, when I'm trying to sort out how to express something, I notice that before my

A time, I frequently feel preoccupied, not at a conscious level, but somewhere deeper. It's a struggling feeling, a cross between wanting to push it out, and not being quite ready. Uncomfortable as it is, I've learnt that this feeling signals that I'm working. When whatever is brewing finally emerges into consciousness, I know it will be just what I want to say. As a writer once said, a lot of writing is about waiting for the moment when you are ready to write. The same is true for Elaborate.

ADVANTAGES OF ELABORATE

• It's quick
Instead of spending a long time slaving over a formal 'first draft', you will find the ideas pouring out of you. Many coachees report that they can elaborate a normal presentation in under 20 minutes.

• It produces high-quality work
Many coachees report that working in this way results in presentations which are surprisingly spicy, punchy, spare and concentrated. That makes the basis of a great presentation.

• It's fun
Getting into flow and working this way is like skiing. You poise yourself at the top of the slope. You know where you are going (down) and you have a route (avoid that bump, go between those trees, aim for that steep bank). You take a breath and launch. Bounce, flex, turn, push, sway, jump – and you're there. Wonderful.

• You'll build a new muscle
Working like this will build your creative muscle. The more you trust yourself, the more you follow the guidelines in

this chapter, the more 'creative' you will discover yourself to be.

Action Step: Use Elaborate widely
Why not try doing all your 'first drafts' of any important communication this way? That may include, depending on your job: pitch documents, reports, complex and/or sensitive emails, contracts.

OUTPUT

At the end of **E**laborate you will have a clear idea of what your presentation will be like. For most of us, that will be some words, some main ideas and topics, an example or two, and the ending. But it may be more wild than that. For one coachee, what had started out – pre-GOER – as a standard team presentation to her boss for the capital to buy some new equipment became a group rap. It was just what she found herself doing at **E**laborate. At the end of this stage she had the idea, the basis for the rap and the beat. That was enough.

Another found herself designing a fully interactive session where the 'audience' became participants. Instead of a presentation, it became a powerful team-building session. By the end of **E**laborate she knew how it started, what the exercises were, and how it would end. She had some words for each bit.

Another coachee at **E**laborate made a link between the process he was describing to his boss and the maturation of a butterfly. He had the main links sorted out between egg, caterpillar, chrysalis and butterfly.

And Mike and David? Here's what they came up with:

1. Introduce the two of them – their careers and backgrounds in terms of their work in the conservatory market. Mention Elderflower and explain how the scandal happened after they both left.
2. Introduce the rest of the Board and the management team.
3. An overview of the conservatory market:
   - what drives consumers
   - customer attitudes
   - overview of suppliers
   - distribution channels
   - product groups.
4. Their business:
   - overview
   - brands
   - facilities.
5. Financials:
   - profits and returns for the last 6 years
   - assets.

And that was it. Their advisers (lawyers and bankers) said they were the best prepared presenters they had ever worked with. The presentations, according to Mike, worked a treat. He apparently enjoyed doing them, as he changed what he said each time, learning from the previous experience. And yes, they did get their money.

SUMMARY

All **Elaborate** really is, is day-dreaming with a purpose. At last, an excuse to do what most of us have loads of practice doing. Sitting and imagining what we want to say. And now all that practice will come in useful. How long will it have taken to get this far? **G**oal – less than an hour. **O**utline – again, less than an hour. **E**laborate – at most half an hour.

All you have to do now is **R**efine and you're done. That's the next stage of GOER.

Refine

5

Two yuppies get married, have kids, discover it doesn't work and get divorced. Ten years later they meet in the first class lounge of a major international airport. He greets her warmly:

'Wow, you look fantastic! Things going well?'

'Never been better. But look at you! Very smart. I assume things are great with you too.'

'Absolutely.'

Long silence.

'How're the kids?'

'Ohmigod. I thought you had them.'

A joke is a kind of presentation. Like any presentation, it is (usually) done aloud, by one person, to a group of equals. It also has an objective – to make the audience laugh. We can use the structure of a joke when considering **R**efine because we all know the difference between a well-told one and one that's not. That's what **R**efine is all about. Taking the material you produced at **E**laborate and honing it into a well-told package, one that hooks the audience in at the start and holds them gripped until the end.

I've distilled the activities involved into the five Rs of **R**efine. They are:

1.   Reduce
2.   Restructure
3.   Recall
4.   Rehearse
5.   Redo

What I recommend is that, initially at any rate, you go through your elaborated presentation several times, thinking of it in a different way on each pass. This will enable you to get it from raw to mature in a surprisingly short time.

The initial pass, Reduce, basically involves chucking stuff out. Since you haven't slaved over anything laboriously, it shouldn't be such agony as it would have been if you had used the School Essay Technique. The Reduce phase is when PowerPoint slides and your handouts appear, if there are going to be any.

The second activity is Restructure. This also usually doesn't take long. It's just a matter of rearranging what you've got left: putting this bit *here*, and that bit *there*.

Now you memorize – in other words, Recall – what you have left. I have learnt a way to memorize a presentation that is quick and easy to do.

Rehearse is self-explanatory. The only difference with GOER is that Recall is a form of rehearsal, so reducing the need to actually do it aloud.

Redo is only necessary for major presentations.

THE TRUTH ABOUT STRUCTURE

For a presentation of any length, the middle is the easiest bit to get right. It contains a lot of material, but all that you have to do is put that in the right order. The end is more difficult. You have to round it off satisfactorily. But, because the middle is mostly sorted, you don't have too many choices. The most difficult bit, by far, is the beginning. It is not unusual for the beginning to be the last bit you manage to get right. So, at **R**efine stage, you may in practice find it easiest to sort out the middle first, then the ending, and only focus on the beginning last. It may seem a bit counter-intuitive to operate that way, but it works for many people.

Let's examine the first activity, Reduce.

1) REDUCE

Two yuppies get married. You know the sort of people I mean. He's got a thrusting jaw and keeps ultra fit – but looks exhausted – and she's good looking in an impressed-with-herself kind of a way. She looks on edge, jumpy – as if she's constantly comparing herself to others – which, of course, is what she's doing. They've got it all, but somehow it doesn't satisfy them and they keep pushing themselves to get more – better jobs, more clothes, another house or two, more cars. Of course, they've got to have kids – a boy and a girl (naturally) – who are bright and good looking too, but somehow brattish, perhaps because Mum and Dad are always working, and they're being brought up by a nanny . . .

How did you feel reading that? Did any of that extra information improve the joke? Personally, I got bored really quickly. In terms of joke telling, that's what someone who can't tell jokes does: adds lots of stuff that amuses them, but which contributes nothing to your experience. Good presentations are to the point, containing only the information that the audience actually wants to know. Reduce consists of going through your presentation slimming it down so that this is what the audience gets.

There is a design principle that I find useful here. It is to remove elements progressively until the sense collapses. You then put back the last thing removed. The product is now as reduced as possible. Remember, you are doing this with your audience in mind. Some audiences – for instance, Germans – like more detail than other audiences – for instance, Americans. Taking that into account, remove anything that is just nice-to-know. Second, take out anything with even the faintest whiff of ulterior purpose, e.g. to show you in a good light, to show how much you know, to prove how smart you are.

Action Step: Remove nice-to-have information
Go through your elaborated presentation ruthlessly. Remove as much as possible that is not need-to-know.

Time now to 'kill your darlings'.

KILL YOUR DARLINGS

'Your darlings' are those parts of your presentation you are most attached to and like best. They are the fine turns of phrase, the funny bits, the wonderful slides. Often you can markedly improve the flow of the entire presentation, and so its impact, simply by removing (killing) them.

Hilary was doing a presentation to a group of businessmen about the importance of financial PR. A young woman, her audience would be mainly middle-aged, self-made men. When elaborating she had come up with something she felt was both witty and vivid. She planned to tell her audience that investors are like mistresses. They need regular gifts to keep them sweet. Financial PR gave them these presents, tit-bits of good news. Oh dear.

At the very least, this was going to put an entirely inappropri-ate thought into the audience's imagination. At the worst, she was going to get invitations to meet some businessmen with the wrong idea about precisely what it was she was say-ing. Once she had run through her presentation without this idea in it, she did admit that it was an improvement. Phew.

The reason that you should always examine your darlings with great scepticism is that, because you love them, there is a tendency to refine the work around them. As the rest of the presentation moves and flexes and beds down, the dar-lings remain stranded in their original position and shape. At its worst, the whole presentation gets skewed just to allow these darlings to be displayed in all their finery.

I find that the psychologically easiest way to 'kill' my darlings is to put them into a file which I usually call 'Bits'. What I tell myself is that I'm not actually losing these precious pearls, I'm just temporarily parking them, perhaps for later use. That seems to make the exercise less painful. I almost never use them.

Action Step: Kill your darlings
Identify any darlings in your presentation. Experiment with moving them to a separate file. Be honest with yourself. Is the presentation better with or without them?

Another way of reducing your presentation is to move some of your information from spoken words into visuals. We have come, at last, to the subject of PowerPoint.

POWERPOINT SLIDES

> Slide 1: Photograph of two yuppies in a bar.

Presenter: Two yuppies get married . . .

> Slide 2: The word 'Married' zips onto the screen from the side.

Presenter: . . . have kids . . .

> Slide 3: First bullet point zips onto screen from the other side:
> * Have kids

Presenter: . . . discover it doesn't work . . .

> Slide 4: Second bullet point dissolves onto screen:
> * Doesn't work

Presenter: . . . and get divorced.

> Slide 5: The image of the yuppies splits in two and each half moves off to the side to reveal the word 'DIVORCE' in the middle.

We've probably all suffered presentations like that, where the presenter has mistaken the fact that you *can* prepare a fancy slide show, for the idea that it is useful to do so. It is not. The slides above added nothing to the information being communicated. Actually, they made the flow harder to follow.

What's useful in a slide?

Broadly, the guidelines are:

1) When you have something to show

Visuals are particularly useful when you want the audience to see something that you cannot otherwise show them. For instance, Mike and David might have wanted potential investors to see their factory. A photograph, displayed as a slide, would have shown it in its full glory. Equally, if they'd wanted to show a new product that wasn't in the catalogue, a slide would have worked. If they had wanted to show the wonderful materials their conservatories are made of, however, it would be better to have actual samples with them for the audience of potential investors to hold and marvel at.

2) When you want everyone to see the same image

Another use of visuals is when you want everyone to focus on the same thing and words alone can't describe it adequately. For instance, you might want everyone to consider the same diagram, or image of a proposed product, or flow chart. However, in some of these cases, a handout might be preferable. Then the audience could make notes on it. We'll come to handouts in a moment.

3) Text

A good rule of thumb is only to put on screen what would fit onto a T-shirt. Any more, and it's either a handout or you've got to work harder to reduce the message.

Advantages of this approach to PowerPoint

Thinking about PowerPoint in this way eliminates at a stroke one of the main time wasters in preparing a presentation. Because, however easy it is to do a simple PowerPoint presentation, it takes a lot of time to get it right. It also eliminates the trap of displacement activity. Some people, when faced with doing a presentation, launch themselves into preparing PowerPoint slides to make themselves feel as if they are doing something towards getting the work done. That's exactly what they are doing. Something.

Remember the first days of desktop publishing? When you got documents ALL *in* different **fonts with BOLD and <u>underlining all over the place</u>**? I suspect we're in a similar period with PowerPoint. Using PowerPoint sparingly in your presentation also avoids the trap of directing the audience's attention away from you to a screen. They are there to connect to you, not to a close up of a buttercup and a screen full of bullet-pointed text.

Action Step: Prepare your PowerPoint slides
If you wish to have slides, begin to assemble the material now.

You may be able to reduce further by moving some information from the spoken word to paper. In other words, create a handout.

HANDOUTS

Personally, I operate on the principle of 'no-one leaves my party without a present'. If I do a presentation, I like to offer the audience something to take away with them. Most people appreciate having a handout to file – even if they never look at it again.

What's in a handout?
Useful material in a handout includes:

- Contact details – email address, websites, phone numbers, etc.

- Supporting evidence for something you mention, such as flow charts, spread sheets, lists, etc.
- Details of case studies you don't need to include in the presentation.
- Technical details you don't need to cover in your presentation.

In other words, the handout is not a self-contained document. It only makes sense by reference to the presentation.

What shouldn't be in a handout?
Your handouts should not be the book of your presentation. The worst case is if your handout is little images of your PowerPoint slides. No-one is interested in this but yourself.

They also shouldn't contain anything that is more interesting than your presentation. If, for instance, you do a presentation that contains anything related to money, and put the budget in the handout, what's going to happen in your presentation? Aren't people going to turn to the last page of the handout and study it, ignoring you? Isn't that what you'd do in their place?

In other words, the handouts should support your presentation, not the other way round.

Action Step: Handouts
Decide whether or not to have handouts. Put any technical material there.

Your presentation may look significantly sparer by now, with some material ready to be in PowerPoint, and other in handouts. Time to fine-tune its structure. To do that, we need to clarify the structure of a presentation.

2) RESTRUCTURE

What's the fundamental structure of any linear communication? It is very simple: beginning, middle, end. When I
first heard this formula, studying English literature in
college, I thought it was one of the most banal things I'd
ever heard. Over the years, I've realized it's actually quite
profound.

Initially, we'll look at it in terms of beginning, then end and
finally middle. What you are aiming to do is improve the
order of ideas within the optimal linear order as decided at
Outline. Resist the temptation to mess with that – it's something your audience have told you works for them, so respect
that and ensure it works.

THE BEGINNING?

What's in a beginning? A good place to start is considering
the joke. Every phrase has its function:

Joke	What's in a beginning?
Two yuppies . . .	Who it's about
. . . get married . . .	What it's about
. . . have kids . . .	The set-up for the pay-off at the end
. . . find it doesn't work . . .	A hint at the meaning
. . . and get divorced.	End of the beginning

All these elements are useful in the beginning of a presentation.

• Introduce yourself

This is essential if you are doing a presentation to an audience that doesn't know you. Explain why you are qualified to speak on the subject. When doing a presentation to colleagues, no need to introduce yourself of course, but it may help if you outline your expertise as it relates to the particular subject you are talking about.

• What it's about

You want to indicate the subject area early on so people can orientate themselves from the outset. You might say 'I'm going to be talking about project management', or 'my concern is project management from the financial point of view'.

• The set-up for the pay-off at the end

This is a technical, writer's trick. We'll examine it later, when we look at how an end works.

• A hint at the meaning

Everything in your presentation will be infused with your meaning – Your Intention. It may not surface explicitly, but it should be there, a subtle and constant presence. In this joke, the off-hand statement 'find it doesn't work' followed by the callous 'and get divorced' expresses the yuppies' values, or lack of them, which is at the core of the humour.

Action Step: Sort out the beginning
Ensure you have all the elements that a beginning needs, and move anything that shouldn't be in it to later in the presentation.

WHAT'S IN AN ENDING?

How does the joke end? What does each phrase do?

Joke	Function of phrase
How're the kids?	Beginning of the end.
Ohmigod. I thought you had them.	The pay-off for the set-up in the beginning

Again, that's it. The ending wraps up the narrative begun in the beginning.

There are several things to say here.

Set-up and pay-off

This is a very effective structure, which you are almost certainly familiar with from television drama. Think of a TV show. The police visit a crime scene: a bicycle courier has been murdered on a busy city street. They cordon off the area, which brings them into conflict with 'typical' city folk – the slightly mad old lady who wants to get back to her flat, the exhausted shop owner who wants to open his place, the bad-tempered newspaper vendor who is going to miss a prime period for sales. They work through the suspects: his bitter girlfriend, his rival couriers, the boss he disrespects. After many twists and turns, the police discover the true villain. It was . . . the newspaper vendor. We accept this because we met the man, albeit briefly, in the opening scenes. The first glimpse of him is 'the set-up'. Imagine the same story if we hadn't met him in the first scene. Suddenly, at the end, the police discover that the courier was killed by someone who hasn't been mentioned in the story, this unknown bloke who sells newspapers. What?

The set-up/pay-off structure works because, at its conclusion, everyone feels the piece has not just stopped, it has ended. It is relatively easy to engineer this into your presentation, as long as you do it *backwards*. That is, you select the pay-off first, then engineer the set-up into the beginning. For example, imagine you are doing a presentation to persuade a budget holder to buy an air conditioner. The unit you propose is best because it solves some issue to do with utilization of office space. If that's your pay-off, your set-up is simply to say something in the beginning that refers to how office space is an important consideration in this situation. Now, when you refer to the unit solving the issue of office space, your audience will feel satisfied.

Action Step: Decide on your set-up and pay-off
Identify a possible pay-off at the ending, and then engineer a set-up in the beginning to work with it.

The end
I distinguish two kinds of endings. I call one 'Bang', the other 'Whisper'.

• Bang
The Bang ending builds to a climax. It often uses a statement with three beats in it to raise energy. People interested in rhetoric call this the 'Rule of Three', and we'll examine it in more detail in the section on middles. Applied to the ending of a presentation, it sounds like this:

'That's the plan I'm recommending. It's efficient, it's cost-effective and – best of all – it's practical!'

The applause won't come – after all, this is a presentation, not a speech – but the energy has built and there'll be silence after that ending. If you were in the audience, how would you feel about posing a question to the presenter after such an ending? Many of us would feel a bit awkward. The end is so big it feels like there's a hill to climb in order to pose a query.

That's when a Bang ending is useful, when you want to DIS-COURAGE questions. You might use it, for instance, when doing a big presentation at a conference; or presenting a message as part of a series of presentations; or when delivering a company message that isn't one you can comment on usefully. (There. It took three sub-clauses to end that sentence in a satisfactory way.) A word of warning here though. If you do get a question after a Bang ending, it may be quite challenging. That's because the sort of person who is willing to hurdle the psychological barrier will be relatively strong-willed and tough – and their question may reflect that.

• Whisper
A Whisper ending is, not surprisingly, the opposite of the Bang. This is when you reach the conclusion and then slow down and simply . . . stop. That's it. Finished. What happens now? The audience sits there in silence.

If you are a skilled presenter, doing this intentionally, you too sit there in silence, comfortable in the knowledge that your silence is going to be like a vacuum, drawing questions out of the audience. With a Whisper ending, the first question you are likely to be asked may be relatively easy, because the person most disturbed by the silence will be someone kind, who will take pity on you. Once that easy question has been asked – and answered skilfully by you – others will follow and you will have successfully changed what was a virtual dialogue into an actual one.

So the Whisper ending is a version of the cliffhanger. It encourages the continuation of the connection you have established through the communication you have just completed. Use it when you want your presentation to be the prelude to a true dialogue.

Action Step: Decide on your ending
Decide the sort of ending you want and tweak your presentation accordingly.

WHAT'S IN A MIDDLE?

Basically . . . everything else. All the stuff of your presentation: the examples, the logical reasoning, the case studies, facts, figures, and so on. In the yuppie joke, the middle has all the material about airport lounges and how are you doing? You might notice, in passing, that this is all flavoured by the meaning of the joke: that yuppies are laughable because they value material success above everything else. That explains the location of the dialogue – the first class lounge of a major international airport. Only successful business folk have access to these. It also explains the stilted dialogue, which focuses only on their status. The Rule of Three is particularly relevant to the middle of a presentation.

The Rule of Three
With anything like case studies, or examples, or testimonials, if you only present one the audience will perceive that as the only one you did. Two, ditto. Four is overkill. Three is perceived as you having done lots, and then artfully picked the three best to present to them. You can, if you want, present one, and refer to two more in the handouts. Three of anything

sounds good: location, location, location. Or 'I've three priorities: education, education, education.' This rhythm is essential for a well-told tale. It's even in the yuppie joke.

He greets her warmly:

'Wow, you look fantastic! Things going well?'

'Never been better. But look at you! Very smart. I assume things are great with you too?'

'Absolutely.'

Long silence.

Three lines of dialogue: it signals to the audience that this section of dialogue is just to stand in for more that you – as an audience – don't need to know and I, as the storyteller, have edited out for you.

Action Step: Apply the Rule of Three
Go through the middle ensuring that you observe the Rule of Three.

Segues
At its best, the middle will have elegant links, not unlike those a DJ constructs when he segues music tracks from one to another, each blending naturally into the next. In a similar way, you will find that one idea often naturally leads into another.

Back to the imaginary air conditioning unit presentation. In the middle you plan to talk about its capital cost (high), its size (small), its efficiency (excellent) and its running costs (low). What order to put them in?

Here's one possible order:

1. capital cost (high)
2. size (small)
3. efficiency (excellent)
4. running costs (low).

You might decide to have them like that, virtually random. But there are some natural links within the information. For instance, you might notice that the ideas fall into two camps: pros and cons. That's a different order.

1. Pros: size, efficiency, running costs.
2. Cons: capital cost.

That's neat.

An alternative order could be its impact this year, and subsequent years.

1. This year: it will consume significant capital budget, but, since it's small, will fit into the space available for it.
2. Future years: its running costs are low.

It's a good idea to play with different ways of ordering information just to see which works best. You may surprise yourself because many subjects have an internal logic that is not necessarily visible until you become really familiar with them.

Action Step: Segues
Go through your presentation looking for natural links and experiment with shuffling the order in the middle until each subject leads sweetly and naturally to the next.

NOTE ON STRUCTURE

Do you recognize the beginning, middle, end structure described above? The beginning with the hint of meaning in it; the middle with lots of meaning in it; the end which pays off on the meaning? It's the old formula beloved of trainers: tell them what you are going to tell them, tell them, tell them what you told them.

This memorable phrase is much misused. It is a vivid description of an effective <u>presentation</u>; it is not a prescription for one. That is, it tells you what a good presentation is like, but doesn't help build one. Failure to understand this distinction is why all too many people do presentations that begin:

'Today I'm going to tell you about . . .'

Noooooo.

SIGNPOSTS

Once you have the basic structure sorted, you can now add signposts: one from beginning to middle, the other from middle to end. These reassure the audience that they are in the hands of a competent storyteller. This is important: after all, your audience are expert in the construction of linear narratives and well versed in the art of storytelling – at least, as an audience. They expect and will appreciate competence from you.

Can you identify the first 'signpost' in the yuppie joke? It's when the pace changes. At the start, it is stately and the information is fed to the audience a step at a time: they get married, have kids, etc. Then it suddenly changes: 'Ten years later.' Ah, says the audience, we've stopped being in the beginning and have moved into the middle. Now we're going to get the bulk of the information.

Action Step: Add a signpost from beginning to middle
Have a look at your presentation. How do you signal to the audience that you've finished the beginning, and have started the middle? It could be a slide (if you are using them), a change of pace, or a phrase such as 'So what does this mean to us?', 'Let's get down to detail?' or some such.

The next signpost is from the middle into the end. Can you see how it's done in the yuppie joke? It's that phrase 'Long silence'. Ah, says the audience, something is about to happen. The pay-off cannot be far away now. And it is, and that pleases them.

Action Step: Add a signpost from middle to end
Review your presentation and ensure you signal the move from the middle into the end in a satisfactory way. It might be done with a slide that repeats one from the start (ideally the signpost slide), or it might be a phrase such as 'In conclusion', or 'So, what does this all mean for us?' A slide with the word 'Summary' would do too. It's a tad blunt, but the audience will get the meaning.

Your presentation should now have a solid beginning, substantial middle and distinct end. At this stage it is worth revisiting the start, as it is very reassuring for a presenter to have the audience lock on from as early in the presentation as possible – and there are several technical ways to do that.

OPENING = HOOK

Many sales people begin their conversations with prospects by seeking agreement on something – anything – and working from that to agreement to buy the product. That's why you frequently find sales people starting a sales conversation with something you can both agree on. 'Terrible weather we're having at the moment, isn't it?' Yup, nod. A recent study has established that if you tell someone something when they are nodding, they believe you more than if you tell them the same thing and they are not doing so.

Stretch
Pay attention to when you nod to encourage others to talk, and notice how others around you nod to encourage you – or someone else – to continue doing so. Notice also those who do not nod (for instance, well-trained buyers may not nod in order to make sales people feel uneasy).

The two techniques that follow guarantee you'll get the audience nodding from the outset.

1) Thought for the day

This is a last-minute technique. You know what you are going to say in your presentation. Let's imagine the air conditioner you favour is a better than average piece of kit, so quite costly.

In the run-up to your presentation, you keep alert for some major news item you can utilize as your hook. A story that catches your eye is an item about buying an expensive sports player. On the day you start with that. 'Isn't it extraordinary

that Manchester United has paid so much for Wayne Striker?'
Most people will have heard the news, and had that thought,
so they'll all nod, yes, it is extraordinary. Now you make a link
to your topic. 'But I suppose he's a capital asset – and he'll
help them win.' That seems a reasonable thought, so you get
another nod.

The audience must by now be thinking 'where's this
going?' Time to answer that. 'It's the same situation with
the Acme Air Conditioning unit I'm proposing we invest
in . . .,' and you are off and running, pointing out that it
will help the team keep cool and so win. With practice,
almost any bit of news can be used as a hook to introduce
almost any presentation.

2) Three-step formula

The other technique is a three-step formula. (I first encountered this idea in the classic book written by Barbara Minto
on how to present thoughts clearly, *The Pyramid Principle*,
published by Prentice Hall, with my edition dated 2002.)

  i) A statement we all know to be true or can agree upon.
 ii) A problem arising from it.
iii) Your solution to the problem – the topic of your
     presentation.

This is easiest to construct backwards. Point three first: the
topic of your presentation?

iii) The reasons to buy the Acme Air Conditioning unit.

So you require a problem, the answer to which is the Acme
Air Conditioning unit. What could that problem be? For
the sake of this example, how about we say the Acme unit

is particularly effective at keeping temperatures at a set level. As a result, it will be ideal to deal with the see-sawing conditions in your mostly glazed, but inadequately sealed, offices. It will keep office workers cool instead of getting hot and sleepy, and warm instead of getting chilled, so will increase productivity and office morale. So the problem is:

ii)   'When the temperature see-saws, our productivity suffers.'

What statement can we all agree on that leads to the problem? Again, there's a myriad, but one could be:

i)   'The temperature of these offices see-saws around.'

If it's true, everyone in the audience will nod enthusiastically.

Putting the three statements together, they work like this:

'The temperature of these offices see-saws around.'

Everyone nods. It does.

'When that happens, we either get hot and sleepy or cold and irritable – and in both cases, productivity suffers.'

Nods all round.

'That's why I'm proposing we consider installing not just any air conditioning unit, but the Acme.'

Ah yes, the Acme. Now why should we install that particular model? And off you go, with the audience a willing and eager partner in the dance. The advantage of this opening is that, as soon as it starts, the audience thinks to themselves: 'this person knows where I live', in the sense that you are speaking directly to their interests, concerns and thoughts. You've established the connection in the first thing you say in the presentation.

AUDIENCE INTELLIGENCE

At college, I acted a bit on stage. I noticed that we would ask those first out as they came back to the wings how the audience were that night. They'd tell us as if the audience was a person: slow, excited, fidgety, dead. That's because, when you are part of an audience, you become an element in a group. What happens, I feel, is something like this.

You and I and others sit down to witness something – like a presentation. The presenter starts. After a moment, we steal a glance at our neighbour. What is their response? If we notice they are interested, it will tend to reinforce our interest. If they are bored, it will give us permission to begin to drift off. We check others quickly. If everyone is interested, we will continue to concentrate. If they are not, we will swiftly zone out. Which is why you want to get those nods and 'uh-huhs' started early. The more you get them, the more the audience will lock on. From then, it's just a case of keeping the dialogue going.

Action Step: Construct an opening
If you feel it will help you, add an opening to the start of your presentation.

That completes Restructure. Time to move on.

3) RECALL

At this point, it is extremely useful to memorize your presentation. When I say this in a workshop, I get groans. Not memorize my presentation! I've got a terrible memory. If it's any consolation, I used to feel that too. However, I discovered that memory, like creativity, is a learnable skill. The more you use it, and the better your techniques, the stronger it gets. And here is a very good technique for memorizing presentations. Many coachees have learnt it, quickly and easily. Before we examine it, what are the benefits of committing your presentation to memory?

SOME BENEFITS OF MEMORIZING A PRESENTATION

Once you have memorized a presentation, it becomes yours in a way that a presentation on paper never does:

1. You can rehearse it whenever you have nothing else to think about: in a traffic jam; waiting for the kettle to boil; while brushing your teeth. Research has shown that mental rehearsal is nearly as effective as actual physical rehearsal. With a memorized presentation you can go through it many, many times, each time slightly strengthening it, and your grip on it, in time that would otherwise not be particularly productive.

2. You can edit it continuously as you mentally rehearse. This ensures the presentation is mature when you do it.

3. Having your presentation in your memory enables you to present it without 'a script', which is a barrier between you and the audience. Imagine the impact you'd have reading a joke off a piece of paper.

4. At some point in most presentations, most of us say something about how this is our idea; or this is our favoured solution; or the proposal we back. If it is 'yours', you surely don't need to have it written down on a piece of paper? If it is supposed to come from the heart, have it by heart.

5. Memorizing a presentation enables you to be flexible when you deliver it. Imagine that the Chair of the meeting has, in introducing you, covered what you were going to say in the opening of your presentation. If you were relying on a script, you'd now need to shuffle it, trying to edit on the fly. With a memorized presentation, you just step into it half-way through and no-one knows that you've done it. Similarly, if the previous presenter doesn't turn up, and you are asked to fill in, no need to linger on one page of script for ages expanding what's there. You simply pause your recall at the appropriate place, add extra material (that you probably edited out at **R**educe), then move on. No-one will know – everyone will simply be impressed with your flexibility and cool.

6. Without a script in your hand, you can make eye contact with your audience, watching for what works and what doesn't, speeding up or slowing down as you sense their interest waxing or waning.

SOME DRAWBACKS OF MEMORIZING A PRESENTATION

I cannot think of any. Except that you have to do it. So here's the technique.

HOW TO MEMORIZE A PRESENTATION

First, don't try to memorize it by brute force. You don't need to trudge through it time and again, point by point, trying to bludgeon it into your head by repetition. That won't work, and will be painful. Instead, what you do is use a series of fixed 'hooks' that already exist in your memory, and hang the presentation on them. In this technique, the 'fixed hooks' are a journey that you know well and love. When you do your presentation to an audience, you mentally travel the journey, encountering the fixed hooks and the images hanging from them. And the beauty of it is that you can use the same journey for all your presentations. (If you want to learn about other memory-strengthening techniques, I first discovered this one in Tony Buzan's excellent book *Use Your Memory* published by BBC Books, my edition being 1994.)

An example will help make this clearer. Here are the first six ideas in Mike's Clearlight Conservatories presentation:

1. Introduce myself – CEO – I'm doing the presentation.
2. Introduce David – CFO – he's answering detailed questions.
3. My experience: 30 years in the industry, working in four of the top companies in the field, leading figure in the industry.
4. David's experience – left Oxford, spell at major accountancy firm, joined us 12 years ago.
5. Talk about the non-Execs and Chairman.
6. Explain the rest of the team – the Board, the senior management . . . .

Written like that, it seems both easy and difficult to memorize. Easy for Mike – after all, he knows this stuff intimately; difficult for anyone else, because it's all so boring. But . . .

• Easy to memorize
That's the whole point. You are talking to the audience about something you know, that they don't, in order to fulfil their objective and at the same time . . . etc. All Mike needs to do in order to present the resume of himself is to remind himself to do it, and that David comes next, and after that comes the non-Execs and the Chairman. The same goes for you when you do your presentations.

• Difficult to memorize because boring
Perhaps the opening of Mike's presentation is boring to you. But, remember, YOU ARE NOT THE AUDIENCE – and Mike is not attempting to entertain them. All he wants to do is communicate the information they need as quickly as possible. To a banker, faced with making a decision about whether or not to invest in these guys and this company, this is compelling stuff – exactly what he or she needs to know. That is the nature of narrow-cast communications: they are not interesting to anyone but the audience for whom they are intended.

Let's get to work memorizing it. In Mike's case the journey he selected was from his office to home. He knew every inch of it and relished it. Where is the start of the journey? Mike felt it was when he stepped into his car in the car park. But that's missing out a lot of the journey, locations that could be useful for memorizing longer presentations. So where did it really start? We established that at the end of the day he would pick his jacket off a coat rack in the corner of the office. This is, for him, the signal that the day's work was done. That's an excellent image to use for this purpose – a defining moment for a busy businessman. So that is where we placed the first image. To remind him he is introducing himself, he thought perhaps he'd put his name here above the coat hook. That's a bit, well – dull. It needs to be made more memorable. You do this by creating a juicier image. After some coaxing, Mike – an avid rugby fan – decided to replace his normal staid jacket with one in his local rugby club's colours, with his name emblazoned across the back. That's absurd, and made him smile – and that's important. Every image should be positive and pleasing. Then, when you're making the mental journey, you will look faintly amused as you imagine these images, and the audience will notice, and relax because you seem relaxed.

Second significant place on his journey? The car park. Wow – that's going too fast, we won't have enough locations to be useful. He imagined in more detail what happened after taking his jacket off the coat hook. He realized he generally paused at the door to his office to glance back at his desk to check that everything was in order. Fine. A good place for an image. The image should remind him of David, and to mention that David's role was to field questions. After some thought, Mike got a lovely image. David, a big, gentle man, in rugby kit, covered in mud, bent over as if ready to tackle someone. It was another slightly absurd image – just what was needed. The tackling posture perfectly expressed David's role for Mike in the presentation.

Next location? Reception – generally not manned by the time he left work, but he always glanced at it. Here he was going to talk about his experience in the industry. How to memorize such a vague concept? It turned out that this was not a problem. Mike had been a huge Jimi Hendrix fan in his youth, and one of his favourite albums and tracks had been '*Are You Experienced?*' So he simply imagined Jimi on the reception counter, coaxing extraordinary sounds from his guitar. He had to include David's experience – he now put David, with long hippy hair, in reception grooving to Jimi. Mike seemed to be enjoying the exercise.

Quick – without reading back, what are the first points that Mike wants to make in his presentation?

- First location – what is it?
- What does Mike do there – and what's he going to say?
- Second location – what is it, what's there, what's the point?
- Third location – what's the subject?

Did you see Mike putting on the jacket in rugby colours – introduce himself – David in rugby gear by the door handle – fielding questions – and Jimi Hendrix on the reception counter with a long-haired accountant getting down? What's the subject here?

By this stage in a workshop, most people have (a) understood the technique and (b) found it virtually impossible NOT to remember the presentation. And it's not even their presentation or journey. So that's the technique.

1. Reduce each idea in the presentation to a 'trigger word' or concept. In the example above, the word 'experience' summed up for Mike that he wanted to sketch out what he'd done in the conservatory business. Personally, I find it helpful to write individual trigger words on numbered and dated Rolodex cards.

2. Assign an image to each trigger word and place it in a location on your chosen journey.

3. First time through will take you (perhaps) 10 minutes, 15 tops.

4. Rerun the journey mentally immediately after you've first decided on the images. Make any that you can't easily remember more memorable. What generally helps here is to make them ruder, bigger or madder. Can't remember David in rugby gear? Have him by the door, with an entire pack of forwards behind him. Can't remember Jimi at reception? Fill the reception area with nubile fans, screaming at him to help them become experienced.

5. Five minutes after ensuring that your images are memorable enough, run the journey mentally again. Do it again (briefly) an hour later, then three hours later, five hours after that, before you go to sleep and in the morning. The entire presentation will now be in your medium-term memory, ready to work with.

Action Step: Memorize your presentation
The steps are:

1. *Reduce to trigger words.*
2. *Assign images to the trigger words in your chosen journey.*
3. *Commit to memory, then check them 5 minutes later, and then at increasing intervals.*

I'm often asked how you can use the same journey for different presentations over and over again without getting confused. The honest answer is, I don't know, I just know that you can. Every time I put a presentation into my mental journey, it lasts there only until I've done the presentation. It seems to be wiped from my memory immediately after use. Here's a practical demonstration of that.

CHANGING YOUR MIND

Let's imagine David falls ill while in the middle of the IPO presentations. So now Mike has got to do the presentation alone. Fine. Forget David by the office door. He's not an adoring fan at reception either. How long did that take to remember? About as long as it took, presumably, to read.

Let's change it more. Imagine Mike now decides he does not want to do the presentations alone, so drafts in Ingrid, the Marketing Director, to help. She'll be able to talk about how the market is developing in detail and how the investment will provide sales opportunities and so on. Let's imagine Ingrid is a fairly glamorous, tough, forty-something. How does Mike remind himself to mention her and what she's doing in the presentation? Easy: put her by the office door in place of David. Her function is to do with the future of the market, so she could be a fortune-teller? Perhaps he mentally clothes her in a black cloak, sitting in front of a crystal ball. Even better, he might surround her with piles of crystal balls which she's selling, on a two-for-one deal. That'll remind him to mention her sales expertise. Of course, she's also got to be placed in the crowd watching Jimi. How about he put her in a totally unsuitable hippy chick outfit, and have her doing one of those embarrassing hippy dances? Done. Need to check that you have remembered that?

This highlights something almost magical about memory. Recalling a memorable image takes about as long as it requires to imagine it.

POWERPOINT

Now you can coordinate your PowerPoint images, if you decide you need them, with the trigger words. If you feel some of your slides are asinine, delete them. The truth is, you do not need slides from beginning to end of a presentation.

I'm not going to write more about PowerPoint here: there are enough books, articles on the web, and advice on that already. At the end of this, you will be left with slides that accompany what you are saying, rather than drive it. They will also serve as a subtle memory prompt.

Action Step: PowerPoint
Create the PowerPoint slide show for your presentation, if any.

Once your presentation is securely memorized, it's time to think about a rehearsal.

4) REHEARSE

Much of your rehearsing is accomplished by running through your memorized presentation.

BENEFITS OF REHEARSING MENTALLY

The most obvious benefit is that you will become better and better at doing your presentation as you rehearse. But you will also be:

i)   *Honing your presentation.* The more often you go through it mentally, the clearer it will be on the day. Phrases will just flow out of you, easily and naturally.

ii) *Building your memory muscle.* The more you memorize, and the more often you memorize, the better your memory will be. A coachee who was worried that his memory had been damaged by enthusiastic use of marijuana in his teen years now regularly memorizes the content of an entire day's workshop with no trouble at all. He says the job takes him 15 minutes the first time through. If he can do it, there's hope for us all!

iii) *Strengthening your creative muscle.* Each time you rehearse, be alert for delightful phrases that jump into your mind, vivid images, captivating links between subjects. Become expert in the use of the Rule of Three: can you add – or take away – something to make a passage work better? The more you use your creativity, the stronger it will become.

Stretch

If you are learning anything new – a sport, a game, some aspect of your work life – experiment with rehearsing it constantly mentally. Note the effect this has on how quickly you improve between practices.

If you are doing a presentation of any importance, it pays to rehearse out loud too.

REHEARSE OUT LOUD

There are several important reasons for this.

- First, and perhaps most important, doing your presentation out loud in its entirety, from beginning to end, will enable you to experience it partly as an audience. You will hear things to change, things that don't work, or could work better.

- Second, you can time it.
- Third, it will test your memory. Intensify the image of anything that you can't remember. Jimi Hendrix at reception with adoring crowds not memorable enough? Make the crowd nude. That should help.
- Finally, you will get used to hearing your own voice.

It's a good idea too to rehearse in front of someone. This will raise your adrenaline levels, so serve as a good dry run. Choose someone you like, who likes you, and ask them for honest feedback. That short-circuits the 'fine, it's excellent' problem. Before you start, explain to them who your audience are so they can understand the presentation. Ask them to be alert to when their interest flags, so that you can address any parts of your presentation that do not seem to be functioning well. Ask them what worked, what they liked, what really landed with them. Often we don't know our own strengths. With this feedback, you can further improve the effectiveness of your presentation.

Spot the problem, don't fix it

Unlike when asking for feedback on your linear orders, feedback at this stage works best when the person tells you what they feel, but doesn't attempt to fix it for you. You should always be the one to fix the problem, otherwise their voice/ideas/take on the world will leak into your presentation, and sit there for ever as an alien lump. This is even true of problems your boss identifies. Establish what they feel needs fixing, then sort it out yourself.

If you've no experience of asking for feedback this way, say it explicitly. It might sound something like this: 'What I'd like to know is what works for you, and what doesn't.' That signals you are not inviting them to brainstorm with you. If they start to get creative with you, smile, thank them, say you will fix it later and ask was there anything else that worked for them, or didn't.

Action Step: Rehearse
Find someone you trust and take a few minutes to do your presentation to them, from memory. Listen to the feedback they give you and act on it.

Stretch
Ask your network whether any of them would like to work with you as your 'R&D' team. These are trusted people who are willing to comment on anything you produce to help you get it right. Send them your ideas, critical documents, CV, etc. and ask them their opinion. This will help you refine everything you produce.

FIXING A PROBLEM: TIP

I've noticed something curious. Sometimes, when there's a problem in a presentation or any other communication, the solution is to examine what leads into it. Sort that out, and I often find the problem magically disappears. Claire, for example, was doing a presentation to live event organizers to persuade them that it was worth taking visitor research seriously. She had a lovely, engaging beginning, a superb signpost into the middle, and the middle was full of strong material. But the end did not work. Her presentation just expired and lay there, cold and unappealing.

A visual person, Claire tried changing the slides at the end to make them jazzier. It was still awful. She tried introducing a Rule of Three ending. Her presentation now climbed, and then fell off a cliff. She tried making it shorter. It now died, abruptly. So we used the tip above to try to discover what was happening. Perhaps it was not the end that was the problem, but the part of the presentation preceding it?

We examined the signpost from the middle to the end. In Claire's case it was a slide saying 'Summary'. Wow, can't you feel your blood racing as you read that? So she put some more thought into it. Her first signpost, from beginning to middle, was sensational. It was a slide that simply said: 'Research is like sex.' That creates a big question in the audience's mind: how so? Answer: if you find research – or sex – boring, it's because you're doing it wrong. So, how could she learn from that signpost, in order to create a better signpost from middle to end?

She came back with a superb solution. It was a screen filled with the logos of major brands. Her point? Sponsorship was, she explained to me, a live event organizer's wet dream (to continue the sexual metaphor). But major sponsors would only invest in live events that are researched in the same way that they research their brands, i.e. thoroughly, professionally and diligently. The ending that followed this signpost was easy now, and flowed neatly to a strongly effective Whisper finish. The proof of the pudding was that after she stopped talking, half a dozen potential clients came to the front to give her their business cards and ask her to contact them.

Action Step: Fix problems

If a part of your presentation isn't working, look at what precedes it. Change that and see if that fixes the problem passage.

LISTEN TO FEEDBACK WITH
THE THREE-LEVEL MODEL

When you get several comments on a presentation, it's worthwhile to listen to the meaning behind them. For instance, one coachee received two comments from different people about her presentation at rehearsal. One told her it contained the right information, in the right order, but was a bit boring. The other told her that the start was too slow, but otherwise it was good. What is the meaning behind that?

It is probably simply that the opening was failing to hook the audience quickly. As a result, the first person wasn't paying enough attention, so found the whole thing 'a bit boring'. My coachee therefore removed the first paragraph of the presentation, and created a different hook. She tried that on a third person. Bingo! Suddenly the whole thing worked.

This – by the way – validates another Hollywood scriptwriter's maxim: start the story as close to the action as possible. Get going quickly. You can give them background (if necessary) and detail (ditto) in the middle, along with all the other information.

It is ideal to do **R**efine over an extended period. Each time you return to your work, you can view it objectively for a short period. As soon as you lose that objectivity, move to another task. In this way, the total time you spend on **R**efine is kept to a minimum.

Stretch
*When you have a communication to do which is critical, construct it, then put it to one side. Return to it later, and do one of the activities in **R**efine (Reduce, Restructure, etc.). Keep doing this till you are*

happy with it. By continually stepping back from it, you will be able to polish it in the shortest amount of time.

And that's it for many workaday presentations. But for a high-stakes one, you may want to go that extra mile.

5) REDO

Imagine you are doing a fairly ordinary presentation to another team about the progress made by your team. It's quite informal. How much time is it worth spending on preparing it? Half an hour? What about if you are doing a presentation to your boss which will affect the course of the next couple of months? How much more important is that to you? Ten times? Then it makes sense to spend ten times as much preparation time on it, perhaps half a day in all.

What about a presentation to a customer that's taken a year of work by the Sales Department to secure? How much more important is that? What about a product launch to your customers – a product that's taken your company years to build? How much more important is that?

For a presentation of critical importance, one of the best things you can do to make it superb is go back to **E**laborate and have another think through it from the start. That's because you'll be elaborating with the benefit of hindsight.

HINDSIGHT AS A PLANNING TOOL

There is an old phrase used to dismiss criticism of something you have done: hindsight is a superb planning tool. Actually, it is true − so exploit it. After all, having got this far you now know:

1. The material you want to communicate.
2. How the beginning might work.
3. How the ending works.
4. What to cover in the middle.
5. All the internal links.

You can now do a superb **E**laborate. Select a period of A time and prepare for it. Something that works for me is to go somewhere different from usual to do this re-imagining. Once you elaborate a second time on this high-stakes presentation, go through the whole of **R**efine again. Get the material fully worked up. And, you know what? If you want to get it really fantastic, go back round the loop AGAIN.

Writing is, as television scriptwriters say, rewriting. Rewriting does not show you cannot write: it shows you are committed to excellence. The top presenters in industry are relentless about this. In their quest for excellence, they re-imagine and re-imagine their presentations. And, by doing it in their minds, not committing it to paper at an inappropriate time, their work does not solidify prematurely.

Action Step: Redo
*If you are doing a high-stakes presentation, return to **E**laborate again and re-imagine it. Enjoy the process. Treat yourself to the best story you can make of your material. Fascinate yourself. You may well be astonished at what you come up with.*

Stretch
Put all your critical emails into Draft the first time you write them. Then, at some later time, polish them. Finally, wait a bit and Redo

them. Compare the edited version, and the rewritten-from-new version. Note the differences.

LEAVE WELL ALONE

And there will come a time when you have done enough. You know what you are going to say. You have refined your slides, if any, so they are simple, clear and communicate precisely what you want. Your handouts, if any, work. Leave it alone now. More fiddling will only spoil it.

SUMMARY

Refine is the longest phase of GOER. But polishing a presentation always takes time, however you prepare it. At least with GOER you know that what you are working on will deliver, and that your labours will be worthwhile.

Time to move on, to consider how you will actually do this presentation.

6 On the Day

Paul hired me to help him deal with his nerves about a presentation. He was a successful businessman who'd built a multi-million pound, worldwide enterprise from scratch. He had also, as a sideline, set up a debating society with a partner, Damian. This was a regular social event, held in a fine hotel's ballroom, where intellectuals, socialites and friends gathered for an evening of talk and socializing. These debates were fast becoming part of London's glitziest social circuit.

Just the week before he'd hired me, Paul had done the initial presentation – almost a speech, but not quite – to the gathering to start the formal proceedings. He told me he was so nervous that his legs had begun to shake uncontrollably. The more he spoke, the worse it got. It got so bad he had to hang on to the lectern to ensure his legs did not give under him. And this a man who was entirely at ease pitching to groups of hard-headed business folk about deals on which perhaps millions of pounds were riding. Could I help? I didn't know, but was – of course – happy to try.

We went through the standard advice to nervous presenters: breathe steadily, focus on friendly faces, and so on. He knew all that. So what was going on? I asked him what he'd actually said. Nothing much, just welcoming those who attended and what he called 'the housekeeping': a request to turn off mobiles, where the fire escapes were, asking them to leave business cards.

What was his intention? Although he didn't know about GOER, he was absolutely clear about this. Up till now, due to Paul's other work commitments, Damian had been kicking off the events with a little welcome speech. As a result, Damian was getting all the glory for setting up such a prestigious venture. Now Paul wanted some of the attention and kudos. What do you notice about what he said in his welcome, and his intention? They are at cross purposes. Who is it who asks guests to turn off their mobiles and points out where the facilities are? The host, or the hired hand?

Paul's words, so reasonable in themselves, were casting him into the role of butler. The more he went on about the house-keeping, the deeper the hole he was digging. His will forced him to keep going – but his whole being was trying to stop him. And being very strong willed, the fight got ferocious. Once he saw this, he was delighted. He hadn't suddenly become neurotic!

We applied GOER to the next address. He called a colleague who regularly attended the events and asked her what she'd like to hear from him and what she'd hate to hear. Simple: welcome to one of the most elite social functions in the city, let's get started. Paul could do THAT presentation, no trouble. I did no more with him.

He was kind enough to send me an email after the next function which he'd hosted. It had been held near the Houses of Parliament, on an evening when the House was in session. Paul had apparently said: 'Welcome to the most important debate happening tonight in Westminster.' He'd got a big laugh, a round of applause, and had sailed through the rest of what he had to say, quite the big man of the evening.

Moral of the story? You are right to be nervous about a presentation if you are using the School Essay Technique to prepare it. But if you have freed yourself from it, you know you are not going to be graded and judged by the audience, so why feel nervous? If you are using GOER, you have talked to the audience about what they want you to say, so have no reason to doubt that your presentation will interest them. You aren't doing a speech, you are just talking, albeit in a special, prepared way. Which brings up the subject of preparing yourself to be looked at.

DRESS CODE

The audience have come to experience you. The way you dress communicates important information about who you are and who you wish to be seen as. Personally, I like to wear clothes that are the same sort as the audience, only – if possible – a bit smarter. If they are dressed in a relaxed and creative manner, I come like that. If they are formal, I come like that too. The mere fact of being looked at freaks some of us out. Time to deal with nerves.

BEING SEEN

A presentation means that you are going to be SEEN. For many of us, we rather like to slide through life – or at least work – without being noticed. When we do a presentation, we are the centre of attention. That causes us to feel alarmed, which means the adrenaline starts to course through our systems. How to deal with that?

Good nerves/bad nerves
The first step is to own your nerves and acknowledge their good intentions. Your anxiety, your raised energy, is there for a purpose. It is to help you perform at your best. And that's important because a presentation, however routine and non-critical, is still a performance. You need the adrenaline that

is produced by nerves – and that produces some of the
unpleasant symptoms of nerves – to crank your system to the
max. Ceasing to fight the adrenaline spike is, in itself, a step
forward. Your energy won't be diverted into a pointless battle.
Second step: find a way to take the edge off the side-effects
of adrenaline.

Action Step: Welcome your nerves

*Think about your nerves. In your own terms, in what way are they
helping you, either now, or in the past? Can you find a form of words
that will acknowledge their good intent?*

*When you next feel nerves before having to say something to a group,
experiment with greeting the nerves and offering them thanks. Notice
how this makes you feel.*

Side-effects of adrenaline

The adrenaline surge all of us feel when we expose ourselves
to the gaze of a group can have any, or all, of the following
effects:

- – A pounding in our heads.
- – Breathlessness.
- – Nausea.
- – Sweating palms.
- – Cold hands and feet.
- – A narrowing of our visual field.
- – The need to gabble to others – or a desire to be by our-
selves.
- – An inability to focus mentally.

The usual advice about how to handle these side-effects is to
breathe, and that is absolutely correct. In principle. The
trouble is, when you are really beginning to panic – which

is what this is – breathing steadily is difficult. With GOER, however, you have an ally, and that is your memorized presentation.

YOUR MEMORIZED PRESENTATION AS MEDITATION

When the panic kicks off, you need to find a way to steady your mind and begin to breathe normally. There is an easy way to do this. Take your prompt cards, list of trigger words – whatever you have to remind yourself of your memorized presentation – sit for a moment and begin your mental journey. You may need to force yourself to focus at first, but it's worth it. Coordinate your images with your breathing. Breathe in: pick up the jacket in rugby club colours off the coat rack. Introduce yourself. Breathe out: pause by the door of the office. Notice David, in rugby kit, surrounded by forwards. Introduce him. Breathe in: reception, Jimi Hendrix on the counter – my experience. Breathe out: David watching Jimi, surrounded by adoring Jimi fans. His experience.

And so you go, stepping through the journey, breathing steadily. You may not get far the first time you do this, but the familiarity of the mental discipline, the routine, will calm your mind surprisingly quickly. The steady breathing will start the process of calming your body. You'll have the benefits of the adrenaline, and will have taken the edge off the nasty side-effects. Don't worry if you can't recall every stage of your journey. In the initial phases of an adrenaline surge, it'll be hard to focus on the whole presentation. That's OK – this is just the start of working with your heightened energy. Some of the following thoughts might also help.

REASONS TO BE CHEERFUL

1) The audience want you to be good
Remember what you're like when in an audience for a presentation. Are you not, in common with most others there, hoping against hope that this will be a good, relevant, interesting presentation? And, if it is, aren't you delighted? In other words, the audience are on your side. They are your allies.

2) The audience have low expectations
What are your audience expecting? They are probably expecting – bracing themselves for – the usual school essay, a mind dump that begins with the chilling words 'Today I'm going to tell you about . . . ' Instead, you are going to interest them from the beginning, hook them in, deliver on their objective, and end in a skilled way. They'll be surprised and delighted. For now, that's your secret. Enjoy it.

3) Your presentation works!
Another consolation with GOER is that you are certain your presentation works. You have checked and possibly co-created the linear order with a member of the audience at Outline. You did a rehearsal and got feedback. You are not delivering to strangers – even if you've never actually met them before.

4) You are ready
When you use the School Essay Technique to prepare a presentation, you are doing just that: preparing the presentation. With GOER, you are preparing *yourself* for the presentation. It is a very different approach. You know the audience, you know that the presentation works, questions and answers are part of the presentation, your nerves are part of the process.

5) You've got plenty of time

Even if the meeting starts late, that's no cause for concern. You planned for this. If it starts early, that's fine too. If people want to know more from you – that's fine too.

6) You don't need the technology to work

Even if you have PowerPoint slides, you're not dependent on them. So if the technology fails (it has been known to happen) that's OK too. And if you do make a mistake, it won't even matter.

MAKING A MISTAKE

We'd all like to do every presentation perfectly. But the truth is, it's surprisingly OK to make a mistake in a presentation. A coachee of mine, Jean, was very nervous about doing presentations, but accepted that GOER would help her. The only trouble was that she was unaccustomed to trusting her memory. She decided to give it a go for one of her not-so-crucial presentations. A good strategy. Half-way through, with it going well, Jean apparently suddenly remembered that she'd forgotten to say something earlier, something that she now had to say if the next bit of the presentation was going to make sense. She briefly panicked, then decided to just own up. She reported that she said something like: 'Sorry, I forgot to mention x when I was talking about y'. She said x, then ploughed on.

At the end, after it was over, Jean asked one of the audience if it was OK that she'd mentioned about forgetting something. 'Did you?' was the response. 'When?' What Jean discovered was that the audience had been so engaged by what she was saying, so involved in the flow of the virtual dialogue, that they hadn't even registered the 'mistake'. It was just another swirl in the flow of information coming at them. So cut yourself some slack. If you forget something, and realize it in your presentation, either leave it out altogether or admit it, add it back in and move on.

If you choose not to mention it, and it was actually important, someone will probably bring it up in questions anyway. After all, you aren't doing a school essay presentation, with everything in it. The audience will probably assume you've taken pity on them and left the information out because it wasn't need-to-have. That may be true too.

In short, experiment with ways of working with – rather than against – your nerves. Discover what works for you. Try to treat your nerves as part of the process. There are a couple of other things you can usefully do.

FEEL THE ROOM

If it's possible, get to the place where you are going to do the presentation early. Feel the room with your whole being. Sit in it for a moment, and extend your energy out into it, as if you were growing a set of gigantic cat's whiskers, letting them delicately probe the room. Then walk round it and let your body decide where to settle down. Are you going to stand or sit? It doesn't matter which – remember, this is an informal communication between equals, not a speech – all that matters is that you are comfortable.

If your presentation is in a meeting room, with a lot of people attending, you can even sort out the audience's chairs in the way you want. Do you want them around a table? Or in groups around separate tables? In a circle? Theatre style in rows? Whatever makes you feel comfortable, do it. The audience, when they walk in, will just accept whatever they find.

If you've got handouts, decide what you want to do with them. Put them in a pile at the front? In front of each person's chair? In a pile in front of you? Out of sight, but within reach?

WARM UP YOUR VOICE

It's a great idea to warm up your voice just before the presentation if you get the chance. Personally, what I do is go to the toilet and hum loudly. Yes, I do feel a bit self-conscious, but the vocal chords are controlled by muscles, and like any muscle, they work better from warm. I sing a bit, and go 'lalalala' loudly several times. Other occupants of the facilities seem to accept my behaviour without comment.

DOING IT

Once you have launched into your presentation, and are doing it, you may find yourself flying – skimming along, buoyed up by your audience's interest and attention, your connection to them, your connection to your subject. It's a lovely feeling, you and they in community. If you notice yourself in this state, relax, enjoy it. You have worked for it. It is now repaying your investment.

IT'S DONE

And, before you know it, it'll be done. Your words will have left your mouth, and it will be over. Now for questions.

QUESTIONS, QUESTIONS

I absolutely loathe the phrase 'dealing with questions'. We *deal with* vermin. We *deal with* terrorism and floods. Questions from an audience aren't like that. They are a sign that you have engaged the audience. That they are interested. So, personally, I welcome questions. That's partly also because of something I noticed when I was younger.

When I started writing for a living, I got it into my head that I wanted to be a feature film script writer. My only excuse is that I was young. Eventually, after much struggle, I managed to get to Hollywood, interested an agent in an idea and my writing, and proceeded to have the whole mad experience – days of driving round LA pitching to producers and meeting them in hotels and restaurants. They were all delightful and encouraging. But none asked me back for a second meeting, the next step in the writer/producer courtship ritual. And then I met a young producer who wasn't so encouraging. He ripped into my story. He grilled me about it, exposing gaping holes in the narrative. I came out of the meeting stunned at having been treated this way, only to be told by my agent that he was really interested in my idea and wanted to see me for a second, follow-up meeting.

I realized then that questions are a sign of interest, and that praise of a certain sort is a way to brush you off without offence. So I urge you to welcome questions. They prove you have connected.

How to answer questions
The most important thing to do is remember the three-level model of listening (Chapter 2: Goal). Listen carefully to

what the questioner says, right up to the end of the question. Listen to every word. Listen to the meaning. If you don't understand, ask questions back. Once you understand the meaning, answer it. In other words, this is your opportunity to turn your virtual dialogue into a real one. And don't be afraid to use the magic phrase 'I don't know'.

I don't know

What do we call someone who knows everything, or – at least – seems to think they do? Isn't it 'a know-all'? That's not a term of approbation, is it? Only strong, confident people can use the phrase 'I don't know'. There are several powerful ways to use it, especially in answer to a question posed to you, a presenter, in front of an audience.

- 'I don't know, but I'll get back to you.'
This extends the connection between you and this member of the audience from the presentation to beyond it. It will cement your relationship.

- 'I don't know, but I can find out.'
You are extending the relationship, and showing your resourcefulness.

- 'I don't know. Do you have any ideas?'
You are showing respect for them, and initiating a dialogue.

- 'I don't know, but perhaps someone else here does.'
You are drawing the whole group into a potential dialogue.

- 'I don't know. What an interesting question. Let's talk about it.'
You are recognizing the value of dialogue, and encouraging it to develop.

All the above, and many more variations on the theme, will help take the dialogue to a deeper level.

Stretch
Pay attention to how people in interviews on television and radio answer questions. Note which ones irritate you, and which you admire. I remember hearing a senior diplomat on a radio interview and it was wonderful. He laughed a lot, kept saying 'I haven't the faintest idea at all' – a lovely, emphatic version of 'I don't know' – and, at the end, had converted what could have been an unpleasant grilling into a sensible, humane analysis of a difficult issue.

SUMMARY

With GOER you are not seeking to be the star pupil, full of knowledge, eager to impress your elders. You are an adult, treating your audience as adults. Nerves, mistakes, an acknowledgement of your perfectly human limitations – all will actually *help* to forge the connection between you and others that is at the heart of a powerful communication. But sometimes, given the realities of modern business, you will not have time for all the preparation work set out in the preceding chapters. You may have to do a presentation unexpectedly. What then? In fact, that's when GOER is particulaly valuable, and it's the subject of the next chapter.

You get an unexpected call from your MD. Some important visitors are here from Head Office. There's been a conversation about Project X which is half-way through its lifecycle. You are the most senior person who knows about the project, so could you come up to the Boardroom in one hour and tell them – the Board of your company, plus the VIPs from Head Office – what the project's about, how you are going to make it happen, and when the benefits will begin to be felt? The clock starts now.

What do you do? You have under an hour in which to construct a presentation. Do you resort to a truncated version of the School Essay Technique because you just don't have time for GOER and all the research and listening it entails? Absolutely not. This is precisely when GOER becomes most valuable. It is, after all, a technique. You have – I hope – practiced it a few times, so are familiar with it, know it works, and have begun to trust yourself and your creative and memory muscles. Time to rely on your skill and really go for it.

What you do in these circumstances is a very pared down version of GOER. Here's how it works.

00.01 GOAL

You call one member of your audience or someone who can model their minds. In the example we're using, you'd probably call someone in your company who is relatively high in the hierarchy and has had plenty of experience working with Head Office and your Board. You quickly explain the situation to them and ask for 5 minutes now to help you prepare the presentation. Given that it is for your Board and Head Office, they'll probably agree to the request.

First step: fill them in about Project X (listen to yourself carefully here, what you say may well be useful for your presentation). Then ask them to put themselves into the shoes of your visitors and tell you:

1. What they would love to hear you talk about.
2. What they would hate to hear you talk about.

Make notes about what they say. Request permission to call them again in (say) 20 or 30 minutes for another 5-minute chat. Find out where they'll be, and the best number to call them on.

00.10 CREATE AN AUDIENCE OBJECTIVE

Think about what you have discovered from your research and distil it into a formal Audience Objective. What do your audience want from your presentation? To . . . ? Perhaps you decide it is something as straightforward as 'To update themselves on the progress of Project X'.

Now establish Your Intention. Apply the Five Whys to the Audience Objective. Go through it swiftly several times just to get perspective and then craft a compact statement. You will hear Your Intention ring true when you say it.

In the example we're using, the first of the Whys is: 'Why do I want to update them on the progress of Project X?' Sidestep the teenage answer ('because they've asked me to') and seek the adult one. What's the reason you – and your team, your department, your bosses – want to update Head Office about Project X? Perhaps it is to continue to get buy-in. Why do you want to get buy-in? Again, sidestep the victim response ('because without it we're sunk') and seek the adult in you. Perhaps it's because their buy-in will allow Project X to continue without interference. Interesting. Why do you want Project X to continue without interference? Perhaps because it's going really well, and interference will slow things down.

The first half of that response is very valuable. The project is going well. That's worth saying. The second half sounds like it could do with more exploration. Why does interference from Head Office slow things down? Perhaps it's because when Head Office interferes – as they did with Project U, V and W – things slow down, and the result is compromised. So perhaps Your Intention is to communicate that Project X is doing very well *because* you've been allowed to get on with it.

Imagine those were your answers to the Five Whys in the situation above. Your presentation has just changed. Ten to twelve minutes work has transformed it from a school child's report to grown-ups about progress, to something much more interesting and substantial.

00.15 OUTLINE

You don't have time for the Dump or Dig spider diagrams. Go straight to the Meaning Generator. Write Your Intention in the middle of the page and generate a whole load of magic words.

In the example we're using, the Meaning Generator might look like this:

Initiatives	Us	Due to	Our company
Other projects	The cause	In spite of	Our department
Development work	Those responsible		Our section
Our expertise	The parent company		Our team
Project X	**is doing well**	**because**	**we've**
been allowed	**to get on**		**with it**
Been able to	To work		Not with reporting
Been trusted to	To develop		With the work
Our track record			With no politics
			Plans
			With our approach

Reading through that, a powerful presentation is rapidly taking shape. Its meaning is something like this:

Our expertise is enabling us – our team, department and company – to do this work which is going to plan partly because you, the parent company, have trusted us to develop the project.

Once you've done this, do the Clarify spider diagram. Write your Audience Objective in the middle of a clean sheet of paper, read through the magic words and, working quickly, sketch out the four main topics you want to cover. Jot down some ideas connected to each and stop.

The four topics on the Clarify spider diagram might be:

1. Progress vs plan.
2. High-level summary need for Project X.
3. Estimated time of delivery vs plan.
4. Benefits Project X will deliver.

00.25 OPTIMAL LINEAR ORDER

Time to sort out the optimal linear order for these subjects. Quickly construct two linear orders and call the person helping you to understand the audience. Pitch both orders to them without indicating which you prefer. Which do *they* prefer? Probe to discover their thinking. Listen carefully to their feedback. Decide – possibly co-create with them – the optimal linear order.

00.30 TIME TO TAKE A BREAK

You need to switch your mind from analytical to creative, ready to do **E**laborate. Take a 5-minute walk, have a cup of tea, gaze out of the window. Whatever will help clear your mind. Do not take calls, do not look at your voicemail or email. Allow your mind to freewheel. You are preparing yourself to create, dahling.

Even in this break, you may well find that your mind is already starting to construct words and phrases for you without your hassling it.

00.35 ELABORATE

Go somewhere you can sit and dream or walk and spend only 5 or 10 minutes elaborating your presentation. How are you going to begin? What are you trying to say? What's the ending? Zip from start to finish in one session in your imagination. Jot a few words or notes to remind yourself of what you have imagined.

00.45 REFINE

You are going to short-circuit the whole of **R**efine by starting with Recall. Trust yourself that you'll easily be able to recall such a simple presentation. Put images into your journey. As you work on Recall, Reduce what you're going to say. Is there a block of technical information? That could be a handout. Someone in the project has just this information already prepared that you can use. Is there something you want them to see? That could be a PowerPoint slide. That too is probably on the system somewhere.

As you work on memorizing, be ruthless about Restructuring. Does your beginning move fast? Can you make it faster? What's the quickest way to get your first nod from your masters and the visiting VIPs? It'll really raise your spirits to get that. Don't worry about signposts or a hook. If they're there, marvellous. If they're not, it doesn't matter.

00.55 REHEARSE

You now have a memorized presentation, with (possibly) a handout and perhaps a PowerPoint slide or two. Go through your Recall again – that is your rehearsal. You are done.

A strong presentation in under an hour. It'll be spare and to the point. It'll have just the information you need in it. It'll have a coherent meaning.

The flow chart below sums up how to use GOER in an emergency.

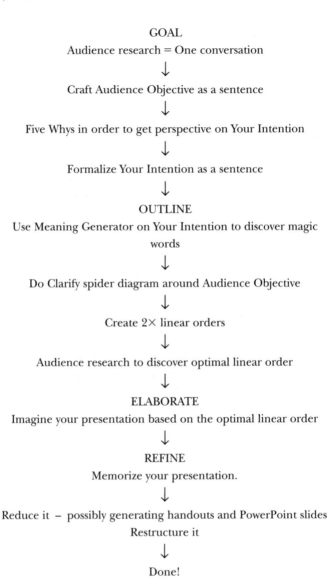

GOAL

Audience research = One conversation

↓

Craft Audience Objective as a sentence

↓

Five Whys in order to get perspective on Your Intention

↓

Formalize Your Intention as a sentence

↓

OUTLINE

Use Meaning Generator on Your Intention to discover magic
words

↓

Do Clarify spider diagram around Audience Objective

↓

Create 2× linear orders

↓

Audience research to discover optimal linear order

↓

ELABORATE

Imagine your presentation based on the optimal linear order

↓

REFINE

Memorize your presentation.

↓

Reduce it − possibly generating handouts and PowerPoint slides
Restructure it

↓

Done!

Once you are used to working in this way, you may even adopt it as your standard way of preparing yourself for a presentation. That's because there are clear advantages to this version of GOER.

ADVANTAGES OF USING
EMERGENCY GOER

- Working in this way is excellent training for both your creative and your memory muscles.
- The result is a communication that is crisp and spare. Audiences usually love that.
- After you've done a quick GOER presentation, having a whole week to prepare one will seem like a luxury.
- It's surprisingly fun to work like this. It's like skiing a steep slope. You contemplate the start, plot the first part of the descent, then launch. You bounce from one leg to another and before you know it, you are down. How exhilarating!
- GOER is a technique, so using it over and over again will enable you to become more skilled with it. The more you practice, the easier it will be.

Personally, if I have to prepare a presentation really quickly, and so have not had time to mature it to my satisfaction in my mind, I now also run through the SUCCES checklist that is in Chip and Dan Heath's splendid book *Made to Stick.*

THE SUCCES FILTER

Made to Stick explores what makes some ideas take hold (that's part of the subtitle). It is not about presentations as such, but is a powerful and new take on communicating in general. The authors propose six qualities which make the communication of an idea sticky. They have devised an acronym for it:

SUCCES =

Simple,

Unexpected,

Concrete,

Credible,

Emotional and

Stories.

Simple? A simple message is one that people will remember. Given that I have produced it with GOER, it usually is. But it is worth asking myself the question.

Unexpected? To what extent am I just trudging through the expected, rather than delivering something fresh?

Concrete? A useful reminder. People remember information that is more than just abstract. If I haven't done so already, I put real examples into anything I present.

Credible? How do you make a presentation credible? Many ways. If I understand the jargon of the people I'm presenting to, I use it. I mention relevant testimonials. I explain any relevant personal experience I've had of their situation.

Emotional? Am I doing more than just stating 'facts'? I run through my presentation quickly to ensure that I've expressed my feelings in it, that I have appealed to the audience's feelings, that I've sought to give them an emotional experience.

Stories? Is there a story that will sum up the point I'm making in my presentation?

I use this formula, like the 'tell them one' discussed in Chapter 5 as a description, not a prescription. That is, I prepare my presentation first, then check it against the list and add bits if necessary (as part of **R**efine) to improve its impact.

In fact, while writing this chapter, when I checked it against the list, I realized it was *not* concrete enough. The first version was entirely theoretical – this is what you do *if* an emergency arises. To sort out the situation, I simply called a contact (thank you Giles!) and he suggested the scenario with the visitors from Head Office. It was obvious, as soon as he made the suggestion, that using it would transform the chapter. I hasten to add that all the stuff about Head Office interfering was entirely my own, albeit informed by years of working with large companies.

In an emergency, when I've hardly had any time to prepare a presentation, I also remind myself that I can't really fail in these circumstances.

REASSURING THOUGHTS

Remind yourself that those who asked you to do a presentation in such a short time know the limitations you are working under. They are going to be pleased if you just talk relatively coherently about the subject for a sufficient amount of time not to embarrass them. After all, that's what most presenters do. You'll do much better than that.

And you *have* spoken to a member of the audience or someone who can model their minds (you have, haven't you!). So you know, to a certain extent, what they care about, what they want to know, and how they think. And you are going to address that. How can you not do well?

LAST THOUGHT BEFORE YOU LAUNCH

Just before you launch into your emergency presentation, remind yourself to go into the room and *listen*. Do not simply enter and start to blab. Spend a moment or two on introductions and on getting comfortable. Listen well when others introduce themselves to you. Remind yourself that attitudes are contagious. If someone feels that they have been listened to, they are likely to respond by listening to you in turn.

AFTER THE EMERGENCY PRESENTATION

You'll earn a great deal of credit with everyone when you pull this off. They'll know you got them out of a hole, and will be correspondingly grateful. Remember to share some of the praise with the person who gave up time to help you do your audience research. Their input is part of how you succeeded, so take care to acknowledge that.

SUMMARY

The success of presentations prepared in an emergency often delights those who do them. It is one of the best presentation-learning lessons you can have. It proves, if you need this sort of proof, that audiences are not interested in suffering a brain dump from you, do not want a carefully crafted school essay, and DO want you to speak to them authentically and simply about what they are interested in. After you've succeeded in preparing a presentation in under an hour, and have done it satisfactorily, and been the hero of the day, you'll never fear a presentation again.

The Truth about Presentations

8

Communications are at the heart of work life. Fundamentally, business is just an exchange between people of services, goods and money. That requires effective communications. And human institutions – commercial, academic, charitable, religious and governmental – are just ways to bring people with specialist knowledge and skills together to work. For them to succeed, they need effective communications. And what are markets if not just huge mechanisms for the exchange of information? When communications work well, business, institutions and markets thrive. When they don't, business, institutions and markets fail – and we all suffer.

Presentations are a vital part of these communications. They are an extraordinarily powerful way, in principle, for one person to communicate with many, integral to the way teams cooperate and complex projects get delivered. Done well, presentations speed the flow of information. Done poorly – done as speeches, or essays – the best they do is clog the workings, impeding communications. At worst, they can send the whole information flow off in the wrong direction.

That is really what this book is about: assisting the flow of information in the workplace. And part of the reason that presentations done with GOER work so well is that they are based on a different psychological attitude from presentations done as speeches.

COMMUNICATION BETWEEN ADULTS

In a psychological sense, a speech – or a presentation done as a speech – is a communication from someone in an adult state, to someone in a child-like one. The speech-maker is the adult who knows something, there to impart knowledge.

The audience are there to receive this knowledge, mere children in a school room. The speech-maker is elevated on a platform, the audience sit at their feet. Physically and psychologically, the speech-maker talks down to the audience.

That is partly what makes so many presentations so irritating. The presenter, by making a quasi-speech, is asserting their superiority over you, the audience. But all that distinguishes them from you is that they know something you don't. But then you know lots they don't, and you are not using that to elevate yourself above them. By contrast, a presentation prepared with GOER puts the presenter and the audience on the same level, both as adults. The presenter has the confidence to ask the audience what they want to hear, and respects them sufficiently to take their answer seriously. The audience senses that respect, and reciprocates it, as adults to a fellow adult. As such, GOER is part of a much larger modern trend.

GOER AND THE DEMOCRATIZATION OF KNOWLEDGE

We are living in a revolution, where we are increasingly encouraged not to be childishly passive, but part of the process. You can see this everywhere. We used to have encyclopaedias. They, the knowledgeable, shared their wisdom with us, the ignorant. It was an adult to child interaction. We now have Wikipedias. We, the knowledgeable ones, share our information with each other.

It's the same with YouTube. It used to be that we, the passive consumer, watched television produced by Them, the broadcasters, the powerful adults. Increasingly, we now watch videos produced by us. We are all, increasingly – in the ugly, newly minted word – 'prosumers', productive consumers.

In the workplace this trend can be seen in 'empowerment', where everyone is encouraged to be their own boss, to take responsibility themselves for what they do. GOER is just part of this trend. And, as an adult, it is for you to make your own GOER.

YOUR OWN GOER

GOER is not a straight-jacket, where you HAVE to do this or that. At its best, it will release you to find your own way of doing presentations, locate your own voice, express yourself in your own style. Everyone who uses GOER uses different parts of it in different ways. That is why you may find the stretches in this book useful. They have been included to help you apply the various tools and techniques beyond the scope of presentations, so that they become part of how you operate more broadly.

Stretch: Develop your own GOER

Decide NOT to do something in this book. If you have found an idea alien to you, simply reject it. One of my coachees, for instance, could not bear not to write his presentation. So he wrote it out, every word of it. He polished it carefully, and took it into the presentation with him. In the end, he told me that he did not actually read it, but it went excellently, and he found having the script in his hands essential to his success. That was his way of implementing GOER, and so was perfectly sensible.

Develop your own GOER. Or, alternatively, if you want to do exactly what has been described here, and not vary it at all, that's OK too. You've rejected this stretch. An excellent move.

Which brings us to an idea I am passionate about. It is related to how we learn and progress.

THE SPIRAL OF LEARNING

At the start of the book, I indicated that I believe that doing presentations is a highly learnable skill. Learning any skill takes you through a cycle of knowing and not knowing. At the start of the cycle, we are like kids watching our parents drive a car. All they seem to do is sit in the front seat and turn the steering wheel. How difficult could that be? That's like watching someone doing a wonderful presentation and assuming that what they are doing is simply 'reading' a 'script' that they 'wrote'. This state of not knowing how to do something, and not knowing that you don't know, is called, in the jargon, 'unconscious incompetence'.

Then you have your first driving lesson, and suddenly realize there's all sorts of other stuff to do in order to drive. You are now in a state called 'conscious incompetence'. You know you don't know. It is, in terms of presentations, like doing a presentation and finding it doesn't work very well when you write an essay and read it to your audience.

The driving lessons are in full swing now. You mutter 'mirror, signal, manoeuvre' every time you pull out. This stage is called 'conscious competence'. If you are starting to implement some of the techniques and tools in this book, you are at that stage with presentations.

And then, one day, you can drive. You no longer need to remind yourself to look in the mirror and signal before you pull out, you just do it. That is called 'unconscious competence'. And one day soon, you will automatically be discussing your forthcoming presentation with your audience, and listening to meaning, and tapping into your creativity easily as you sense yourself able to go into flow without a problem.

This model is often called 'the ladder of learning'. Personally, however, I do not see it as a ladder, but as a spiral, the shape you'd get if you traced your finger up the outside of a spinning ice cream cone. Let's start with a person who can drive, halfway up the spiral. Imagine we now magically transport them, and their car, to a deserted airfield and put a police driver skilled in diplomat protection into the passenger seat. The police driver asks the unconsciously competent driver to speed forward and evade a car chasing them. When the officer gives the signal, the driver is to execute a J turn and speed back the way they came without hitting the other vehicle. Oops, there's more to this driving lark than meets the eye. Back to conscious incompetence. That's another turn up the spiral.

They complete the defensive driving training and now feel they've truly mastered driving. Another turn up the spiral. At which point, we transport them back to the deserted airfield and magic a stunt driver into their passenger seat. This time they are asked to drive the car at a couple of trucks racing towards them, hit a ramp at speed, control the car as it turns sideways onto two wheels, and slide it, still on its side, between the oncoming vehicles. Back to unconscious incompetence. Another turn up the spiral.

To me, this is one of the absolute delights of life. At any point in our learning, we are simultaneously knowledgeable and able to learn a huge amount. Unconscious competence is, at the same time, unconscious incompetence. As we journey up the spiral, we know more, and we are ready to learn more. It's a never-ending journey of discovery towards mastery. So this book, and GOER, are not end-points.

They are – I hope – a way for you to constantly upgrade your skills. Here are a few ideas about how to do that.

Becoming more masterful at presentations
Merely being interested in the subject will quickly raise your game. Also, if you encounter someone who does great, natural-seeming presentations that connect – not presentations as speeches – be interested in what they are doing, and how they are doing it. What can you learn from them? You might even try to discuss with them how they approach presentations.

Becoming more masterful at listening
Again, being interested in the subject is, in itself, a way to accelerate your learning. When you notice someone who is particularly skilled at listening, and does it in a powerful way, ask yourself what it is that they are doing. What is it about them that makes others feel safe to talk deeply? You might even seek an opportunity to engage with them one on one, to feel what it is like to be listened to by them deeply, to explore with them your own listening.

If you get really interested in listening, you might consider hiring a coach if you do not already have one. Coaches are trained in listening, and can model good practice for you.

Becoming more masterful at expressing yourself
If you want to become more skilled at the creative part of presentations, you might consider reading a lot of fiction, and writing too. The reading will expand your vocabulary and sympathies, as you live the lives of others at one remove. The writing, especially if you use GOER to do it, will help you discover your individual voice.

There are many exciting ways to write. One coachee wrote about her hobby for fellow enthusiasts and posted on a blog.

Blogs are good vehicles for self-expression because they are informal, and not read by too many people, with little or nothing commercial riding on their success or otherwise. Another coachee wrote articles for his local paper on an issue he was passionate about. Whatever way you choose to do it, writing, and having other people read what you write, is a fine way to develop your personal style of expression.

Becoming more masterful at questions and answers

This is a vital part of presentations as described in this book. To improve the way you answer questions, pay attention to how people interviewed on radio and television do it, especially in news programmes. When someone answers well, and creates a good impression on you, what are they doing that works? When someone answers in a way that raises your hackles, what are they doing badly? What do you want to do more of when you answer questions yourself? What do you want to do less of? Focusing on this skill in this way will not take any extra time, but will help you become more skilled at using audience questions as a way of deepening the dialogue between you and them.

Action Steps: Becoming masterful

Directing your attention to these different subjects will enable you to continue the journey you have started towards becoming a more masterful presenter.

And a word more about something that troubles many of those I coach and train.

Humour in presentations

I hope you have found this book pleasantly lively, perhaps even mildly humorous. If so, it's because I've told the truth.

My truth. That's all I've done. What I have noticed with GOER is that it encourages people to do that. And when we tell others the truth – our truth – they often laugh. It is a special laugh, one of recognition. Yes, they are saying, that's it! I feel that too, but have not heard it said out loud before, at least not in quite the way you are saying it. And this laugh forms a powerful connection between presenter and audience.

But where I have tried to be funny, I've had to take that out at **R**efine, recognizing those bits as places I have strained for humour. Quite often they were my 'darlings', the passages I was most delighted with – best relegated to my 'Bits' file, to languish there till I find a use for them, which is possibly going to be never.

Action Step: Listen for the laugh of recognition
Be alert to the laugh of recognition, in yourself and others. Notice how it strengthens the bond between people. When you next do a presentation, say your truth out loud. Note how the audience respond.

Stretch
When a truth, your truth, pops into your mind, experiment with saying it, even when not in a presentation. See what reaction it generates in others.

Your increasing awareness of this source of laughter will help you make your presentations full of humour, warmth and humanity, while still remaining entirely serious. This is a delightful paradox. The more serious you are, and the more you tell the truth – your truth – the lighter and funnier your presentations will be. Which brings us to another, deeper, paradox.

THE TRUTH ABOUT
I HATE PRESENTATIONS

There are at least three meanings to the phrase *I Hate Presentations*. One is a personal statement. I do, sincerely, loathe having my precious life wasted listening to a poor workplace presentation made inappropriately by someone talking down to me, attempting to prove to me that they are smart and know lots about their subject. Boooorrrring. Then there is putting words to the feelings of others who similarly hate listening to presentations and fear doing them. The final meaning is revealed once you cease to fear and hate presentations. It is the realization that many, perhaps most, presentations in the workplace should not be done at all – or, at best, should be done in a completely different way.

That's because, the more you free yourself from the School Essay Technique and become an excellent presenter, the more you may discover – as many of my coachees report they do – that you do fewer, not more, presentations in the sense that most people mean them. That may seem counter-intuitive, but it's true. Normally, if you've not done something because you felt unable to do it well – like dancing, or singing – once you learn to do it, you do it a lot. But not with presentations and GOER. And there is a powerful reason for this that involves what happens when you focus on a negative.

Focusing on a negative
When you have an issue with something, sorting that issue out can come to dominate your attention. It's like being a spotty teenager. I was that teenager. I was sure my spots were the reason I didn't have a girlfriend. Sort out my spots, and I'd sort out my love life, or lack of it. I did everything to get rid of the little blighters. I washed and picked them, used ointments and lotions. To no avail. It was only some years

later, when my love life had started, that a girl told me the truth. She – and most of her friends – didn't mind spotty boys. Most boys were spotty. In fact, she found boys' spottiness rather endearing.

I realized then that it was not my spots that had prevented me having a love life – it was the fact that I did not go anywhere I might meet girls ('I can't go out, I'm so spotty') and when I did meet them, focused so hard on trying not to let them see the latest whopper that I failed to notice the encouraging signals they may have been sending me. Obsessed with the negative, I failed to interact with life.

It's like that for many people with presentations. When you think you can't do them, they assume mythic proportions, and you begin to believe they are The Answer. If only you were good at them, life would be so much better. In a way, it's true. Not having spots – not being terrified of presentations – is better than the reverse. But merely not having spots – and merely being a skilled presenter – is not the total answer.

LIMITS OF THE POWER
OF A PRESENTATION

I've frequently been in wonderful pitches where the person presenting has done an excellent communication job, and not got the assignment. That can be for all sorts of reasons: the price was wrong, their approach (while crystal clear) did not sit well with the team, another party they were in competition with was even better. So, while it is immensely important to become a skilled presenter – it ensures you get your message across – it will not guarantee that every time you do a presentation, you succeed in persuading the audience to do whatever you wish them to. But it's also worth noting that, once you become a skilled presenter, the very notion of a presentation may change for you.

That's because you will discover, through GOER and the research that goes with it, that the request for you to do a presentation is not necessarily a request for you to stand and talk for 20 minutes. Hard as it is to do that sort of presentation, it is in many situations actually a lazy response. You are really being asked to communicate something to others. It may possibly be appropriate for you to do a conventional presentation, but equally it may not be.

NOT A PRESENTATION

Examples of how GOER results in something other than a presentation are sprinkled throughout this book. Laura, the banker in Chapter 2, discovered that the stakeholders in the meeting did not want her to talk at them, they wanted instead to take advantage of the fact that they were all gathered in the room to share their thoughts and feelings with each other. Vanessa, in Chapter 4, discovered that her presentation would be better as a team-building session. Paul, in Chapter 6, turned his dreary welcome presentation into an opportunity to strut his stuff.

Here are some more examples of this, not from my experience, but from the world in general. I doubt the people involved used the GOER process, but – however they got to the result – they did get there, and it worked.

On a television programme, *Dragon's Den*, in which business hopefuls pitch to wealthy investors, someone came in and sang about his product, accompanying himself on his guitar.

He talked a bit, let the potential investors sample his product, muddled charmingly through most of the answers – and got his money.

In the bid to win the right to host the 2012 Olympics, London wanted to stress that if awarded the prize, the focus would be on children and the bringing together of the world's many ethnic groups. So they shipped a whole group of multi-ethnic kids to the presentation. Point made.

There is a story about an occasion when the British Rail Board attended a presentation by an advertising agency who were pitching for their (enormous) account. The receptionist was off-hand, the reception area untidy, the visitors were not offered tea. They were kept waiting, with the receptionist occasionally telling them it would not be long before the creative team were ready to see them, and then further long periods of waiting. Finally, furious, the British Rail representatives demanded to see the MD of the company. They were shown up to a room where the people from the advertising agency met them. 'You now know how your customers feel about your service. We're going to help you change that.' Apparently, this wonderfully creative and courageous presentation won the advertising agency the account.

Here are some other examples. One team decided not to do a presentation, but instead stage an Open Day. They simply invited people in other departments to visit them and experience what they did. Another realized that what was really needed was an extended conversation before the presentation. Everything was tied up in the course of this conversation – which turned into a negotiation – and, in the end, the 'presentation' was redundant.

My favourite personal illustration of this was done by Chrissie, a client who works for a vast company. She was a Chief Technology Officer at country level. Bright, ambitious and energetic, she was tasked by the worldwide Board to investigate how their computer infrastructure could be rationalized. It was a major project, which had to be done in secret. And then came the time to present her conclusions to the Board. It was a great opportunity, but quite nerve-wracking. She had an hour's slot, and we applied GOER to her presentation. The Board was notorious for wanting information, and lots of it, so she diligently created a massive presentation, at least 30 minutes long, perhaps slightly more, of densely argued material supported by copious PowerPoint slides. But, at **G**oal, Chrissie had also established that what *she* most wanted from the Board was a decision. With their hunger for facts and figures, the Board were notorious for getting stuck in long and inappropriately detailed discussions. As a result, decisions frequently got postponed and it was quite usual for a sub-committee to be appointed to recommend options for action. That just condemned projects to paralysis through analysis. Chrissie wanted to avoid this. As with most Boards, the presentation had to be with the Secretariat two working weeks before the meeting, so she knew that its members would have looked at her work before attending, She called me afterwards to report that the presentation had been a complete success. On the day, emboldened by GOER, she had gone to the meeting, introduced herself, and said: 'I assume you have all read my presentation?' Nods all round. 'Any questions?' That was it. Her presentation was done. A spirited discussion then followed, which ran for almost the whole hour. A decision was made. Afterwards, Chrissie was heartily congratulated by several Board members for her excellent use of time. She got a significant promotion just months later. Now, that's a presentation not to hate.

Afterword

GOER AND COMMUNICATIONS OTHER THAN PRESENTATIONS

The four-stage process that is GOER formalizes a number of different ways of thinking that will help you become a more powerful communicator all round.

GOAL	Based on listening to others and yourself. Analytical.
OUTLINE	Based on listening to yourself primarily, but also to others. You to act as consultant, considering many different ways to achieve an end, and deciding on the best way forward.
ELABORATE	Creative and subjective: trusting and listening to yourself.
REFINE	Critical and objective: examining what you have produced from a third party's point of view.

You can apply this to a wide range of communications, including:

• Emails

Essentially a verbal communication, in text.

GOAL	Focus on Your Intention. What do you actually want to achieve with this email?
OUTLINE	With an email of any complexity, I find it useful to do a quick Spider diagram.
ELABORATE	With email, it is essential to get the right tone, which is usually breezy but not too off-hand. Personally, I write the most critical emails only in my A time.
REFINE	I never send a critical email after I've written it, but instead save it to Drafts. I then get it out some time later and read it as if I'm the person receiving it. I focus particularly on Reduce – the shorter the email, the more likely it'll be read.

• Telephone calls

We've all had telephone calls to make which we know are of some importance. GOER helps with these too.

GOAL	Focus on Your Intention.
OUTLINE	Do several spider diagrams, imagining the conversation going in different directions. Identify in particular what you do NOT want to say. This is often more important than what you do want to say.
ELABORATE	Day-dream it through a few times.
REFINE	When you are ready, just do it.

• **Reports**

GOAL	Audience research is vital. What does the reader/person commissioning it want? A summary at the end or at the beginning? That you use the standard format? Copious background and context? One concise page?
OUTLINE	Spider diagrams are a huge help here to organize what can be a lot of material. Get a big piece of paper if there is a lot of information to cover, or use several sheets. Spend enough time planning it to make Elaborate as easy as possible.
ELABORATE	Block time in your diary for a whole series of short A time sessions. Be realistic. Once you have established a schedule, do your best to stick to it.
REFINE	Proportionally, the shorter the piece required, the longer you will have to spend on Refine. As Mark Twain said, 'I didn't have time to write a short letter, so I wrote a long one instead'.

• **Pitches**

GOAL	Never enter a room for a pitch without talking to someone who can accurately model the mind of those you are pitching to.
OUTLINE	Whatever you say, keep it short. Remember, you are aiming just to say what they are interested in hearing. It's absolutely not about what you are interested in saying.
ELABORATE	Do it in A time and be ruthless. You are unlikely to be the only one pitching, so express yourself pithily, and leave as much time as possible for interaction.
REFINE	For most pitches, Reduce, Reduce, Reduce.

Then go in, and listen.

• Meetings

GOAL	Sort out Their Objective, and Your Intention. Use the Five Whys several times to really be sure you do not head down the wrong path.
OUTLINE	It's often a good idea to have stuff with you in case you need to show it to them, but to have relatively little you actually have to say. Listening is the key activity in most meetings.
ELABORATE	Just work out how to introduce yourself. The rest is down to how the interaction plays out. As they say in warfare, 'no plan survives first contact with the enemy'. The people you are meeting are not your enemies, but the principle is the same.
REFINE	Your introduction of yourself should be meaningful to those you are meeting. Ask yourself how best to make it work for them.

The more you practice these skills, the easier they will become, and the more powerful all your interactions with others will be.

Final Thought

If this book has been useful for you, please give it to someone else. Not because they're bad at presentations – no-one
likes to be told that, however nicely it is put – but because
they could so easily be better at them. The more people do
not make speeches in the workplace, do not write school
essays when they could be communicating in a more appropriate manner, listen deeply and talk about meaning, the
better all our lives will be. We can all be part of shaping and
creating a happier world. Passing this book along will be a
small, but I hope significant, contribution to that.

GOER Flow Chart

GOAL	Research **Audience Objective** ▼ Establish **Your Intention** using the **Five Whys** ▼ Decide on **Action at End**, if any ▼ Define true **Duration** ▼ Establish **Critical Path** ▼ Speak to your **Team**, if any ▼ Get input from the person who has **Approval** if any ▼
OUTLINE	Do **Dump** spider diagram ▼ Do **Dig** spider diagram ▼ Use **Meaning Generator** to surface meaning ▼ Do **Clarify** spider diagram ▼ Establish 2 × **Linear Orders** ▼ Research **Linear Orders** with audience ▼ Establish **Optimal Linear Order** ▼

ELABORATE	Exile the critic and do only in **A Time**. ▼
REFINE	**Recall** ▼ Prepare **PowerPoint** (if any) around trigger words ▼ **Reduce** ▼ Start work on **Handouts** ▼ **Rehearse** ▼ **Restructure** ▼ **Rewrite**? – loop back to **Elaborate**

Ready to deliver!

GOER Check List

	Tick box
GOAL	
Research **Audience Objective** with at least one member of the audience, or someone who can model their mind	
Construct **Audience Objective**	
Use the Five Whys to construct **Your Intention**	
Decide on **Action at End**, if any	
Decide on a realistic **Duration**	
Communicate your strategy to your **Boss** for buy-in	
Decide when to do **Elaborate**	
Set a realistic deadline to start and complete **Visual Aids**	
Set a realistic deadline to start and complete **Handouts**	
Involve your **Team**	
OUTLINE	
Do **Dump** spider diagram	
Do **Dig** spider diagram	
Use **Meaning Generator** to surface meanings	
Do **Clarify** spider diagram	
Establish 2 × **Linear Orders**	
Research **Linear Orders** with audience and decide outline	
ELABORATE	
Book enough **A Time** to do the whole presentation	
Complete the presentation in whatever form is appropriate	
Transfer to computer if appropriate	
REFINE	
Memorize	
Prepare **PowerPoint** (if any) around trigger words	
Reduce	
Start work on **Handouts**	
Rehearse at least once	
Restructure	
Rewrite if the presentation is critical	

Ready to deliver!

Index